The Ballykissangel
Cookbook

The Ballykissangel
Cookbook

Aidan Dempsey

HEADLINE

To my wife Susan and my three daughters Sarah, Rachel and Ruth, whose patience and understanding enabled me to finish this book.

ACKNOWLEDGEMENTS

With special thanks to Susan and Ian Fleming, whose encouragement and expertise were invaluable in the writing of this book. Thanks also to Suzanne Ross-Bain for getting things moving, and to the cast and crew of *Ballykissangel*, Mike Watts at World Productions and Jamie Munro and Julie Cullingworth at BBC Television.

First published in 1998
by HEADLINE BOOK PUBLISHING

10 9 8 7 6 5 4 3 2 1

British Library Cataloguing in Publication Data

Dempsey, Aidan
The Ballykissangel cookbook
1. Ballykissangel (Television program) 2. Cookery, Irish
I. Title
641.5'9415

ISBN 0 7472 2107 3

Designed by Isobel Gillan

Printed and bound in Italy by Canale & C. S.p.A.

HEADLINE BOOK PUBLISHING
A division of Hodder Headline PLC
338 Euston Road
London NW1 3BH

Contents

Introduction

Welcome to *Ballykissangel* country, County Wicklow – also known as the Garden of Ireland – where I have happily spent most of my life. Although I was born in Dublin, it was in Wicklow that my parents settled, where I grew up, and where I first learned to cook. This book of Irish recipes, a distillation of ideas gathered over many years, is a form of homage to that Wicklow childhood.

Traditional Irish cooking is honest and straightforward, using local, seasonal and first-class fresh ingredients. Although she frequently had to make do with very little, my mother cooked in this way, and more often than not, she could turn something apparently uninspiring into food that was nourishing and tasty. From her I learned most of what I know today. Childhood for my five sisters and myself was intimately associated with food anyway; living in the country, and not too far from the sea, we cleaned out byres and pigsties, milked cows, searched for eggs and fed chickens, pulled potatoes, collected berries and nuts, and foraged for cockles and mussels along the beach when the tide was out.

Despite that number of sisters, I was the one, from the age of six, who most often prepared meals for the family – simple suppers usually involving eggs or potatoes. At the age of fifteen I took over completely for two years when my mother was ill. This early training stood me in good stead when I set off on my motorbike to see the world, exploring France, picking grapes and helping in restaurants, and always eating, watching, learning. By the time my wife Susan and I returned to Ireland, we were confident enough to start a catering business. This opened many doors for us and soon we had gained a reputation and were much in demand. We worked from home and catered for all occasions from breakfast in bed for two to sit-down banquets for 500 people, and just about everything in between – weddings, funerals, christenings, corporate entertaining. But after ten years and three beautiful children we decided to spend more time with our daughters and less time with the food. So we bought a dilapidated old coaching inn on the Dublin to Wexford road, a mile or so from the village of Avoca (the real-life *Ballykissangel*), and converted it into a bed and breakfast business. However, with the wealth of wonderful produce available in the Vale of Avoca, it wasn't long before I found myself back in the kitchen, and we opened a restaurant at The Old Coach House.

I am now cooking full time again, and enjoying every minute, taking pheasant and pigeon from Avoca gamekeepers, bacon and pork from the local butcher, gathering wild mushrooms and berries from the forests and hedgerows, buying fresh eggs, cream and chicken from local farmers' wives, and trout, salmon and a bounty of other seafood from coastal fishermen. My cooking is still traditionally Irish to a great extent, but I have adapted many recipes, bringing them up to date, more in tune with today's tastes.

And it was through the restaurant and my cooking that I first encountered the team who make *Ballykissangel*. We have catered for the unit, we have organised parties (Spanish one year, Italian the next), helped in any number of celebrations, put them up, calmed them down, and got to know them all. The three children, Susan and I have even appeared as extras, and if you don't blink, you might see me milling about in a crowd somewhere!

Traditional Irish cooking and the fine ingredients available locally may have been my first inspiration for writing this book, but *Ballykissangel* itself has been very influential as well. The naturalness and wholesomeness of the programme reflect an essential part of Ireland's character, and I hope I have managed to capture some of that, along with some of its gentle wit, in the recipes and ideas that follow.

from the
MOUNTAINS

There are some thirty miles of mountains in Wicklow. Those that live in Dublin claim them to be the Dublin Mountains, but to us, of course, they're correctly the Wicklow Mountains. It's here that they've been making a large number of cinema and television films, among them *Excalibur* and, more recently, *Braveheart* and *St Ives*.

The mountains are covered with fragrant purply-pink heather, amongst which you'll find fraughan (pronounced 'frockan'), which are wild bilberries or blueberries. In this abundant habitat live many potential food animals and birds. There are so many rabbits that you have to watch your step when walking, because of the hundreds of rabbit holes. They're shot by the local gamekeepers, as are deer. Fallow deer were introduced in the twelfth and thirteenth centuries, and sika were introduced to County Wicklow by Lord Powerscourt in the nineteenth. Red deer have roamed wild for thousands of years, and there is said to be a herd of 800 of them in the mountains; if you go looking for them you'll never see them, but when it's dry (and that's not very often in Ireland), they can be spotted early in the morning coming down to the river for a drink.

Woodcock, snipe and wild geese – which fly in to feed and rest in the lakes – are shot in the mountains. The famous Wicklow sheep also live up there, amongst the heather. When the lambs are over six months old (when they are known as hoggets), they're taken up into the mountains to graze. This gives their flesh the maturity of mutton and the flavour of the heather and other wild herbs. When *Ballykissangel* hill farmer Eamonn Byrne heard about a satellite that counted sheep, he had a stark vision of his EU subsidy vanishing. Eamonn expanded his small flock of Wicklows overnight, using home-made wooden sheep distributed across the slopes above the village!

Man-made features in the Vale of Avoca are huge chimney stacks, remnants of the copper and sulphur mining that brought a thousand men and their families to the area during the nineteenth century (the last mine closed in 1982). The traditional miner's lunch would have been a flask of cold tea or buttermilk, a sandwich made from thick slices of soda bread with butter or bacon; and a typical ending to this meal would be, in summer, a large slice of fraughan pie (see page 18).

Poached Eggs on Toasted Soda Bread

*I*n early summer farmed goose eggs are plentiful in Wicklow, and they make a nice change to your chicken egg. Although cooked in the same way, the taste and consistency of the eggs are quite different. I like to serve them on toasted brown soda bread, an ideal light lunch on warm summer days. A fresh free-range hen or duck egg can be substituted.

Per person

1 goose (hen or duck) egg

1 tsp white wine vinegar

2 slices Soda Bread with Hazelnuts, toasted (see page 69)

Irish butter

1 tsp balsamic vinegar

salt and pepper

In your poaching pan, boil 1½ pints (900 ml) water. When boiled, add the white wine vinegar and reduce the heat. (This vinegared water will suffice for as many eggs as you want to cook.) Carefully crack in and submerge the egg in the liquid, and allow to set, about 4 minutes (less for smaller eggs).

Remove the egg from the liquid and arrange on buttered toast. Pour over the balsamic vinegar, and season with salt and pepper to taste.

If you never had goose eggs before, you'll certainly want to get cracking on this recipe!

Roast Leg of Mutton with Stuffed Onions

The life cycle of the sheep can be simply explained as lamb to hogget (from six months), and hogget to mutton (two years plus). The hoggets are put to graze on the mountainside until they become fully grown, usually two years. During this time, the colour of the meat changes from pink to red to blue red, even darker than beef, the colour of good mutton. The fat should be snow white. The traditional ways of cooking mutton are still the best – slow boiling and slow roasting – both of which soften the fibres and make the meat more tender.

These stuffed onions make a good accompaniment to roast lamb as well.

Bone, roll and weigh the joint, or ask your local butcher to do this. Preheat the oven to 180°C/350°F/Gas 4, and melt the dripping or goose fat in a roasting tray. Add the mutton and baste. To calculate the cooking time, allow 40 minutes per pound (450 g) plus 30 minutes over; baste every 20 minutes.

While the joint is cooking, boil the onions in salted water for 30 minutes or until soft. Remove from the water, drain and allow to cool.

Mix the sausagemeat, breadcrumbs, cheese and butter in a large mixing bowl. Season with salt and pepper. Remove the centre from each onion and carefully fill the spaces with the sausage mixture. Bake in the oven for the last 30 minutes of the mutton cooking time.

Remove the mutton from the oven and allow to stand for 15 minutes. Carve into thick slices and serve with the stuffed onions, boiled potatoes and a thin gravy. A feast on a plate.

Serves 4

1 leg of Irish mutton
1 oz (25 g) beef
    dripping or goose fat
4 medium onions,
    peeled
salt and pepper
2 oz (55 g) sausagemeat
2 oz (55 g) fresh
    breadcrumbs
2 oz (55 g) red
    Cheddar cheese,
    grated
1 oz (25 g) Irish butter

Marinated Rabbit with Baby Roast Potatoes

*R*abbits were introduced to Ireland in the twelfth century, and they are a pest in the Wicklow Mountains, almost as much of an embarrassment as the pheasants (see page 60). In the past they were good fare, though, when alternative meats were not available.

When we all lived at home, my sisters would not eat rabbit, so quite often we had what my mother called 'five-legged chicken' in a casserole. The deceit was achieved by soaking the rabbit pieces in cold water for 2–3 hours to whiten the meat. To the untrained eyes of my sisters it would look like chicken!

Serves 4

2 good-sized rabbits

4 oz (110 g) breadcrumbs

2 garlic cloves, crushed

2 tbsp plain flour

salt and pepper

MARINADE

¼ pint (150 ml) white wine

3 tbsp lemon juice, plus
    grated rind of 1 lemon

3 tsp light brown sugar

2 bay leaves

a pinch of dried tarragon

a few chive stalks

½ pint (300 ml) corn oil

POTATOES

2 lb (900 g) potatoes

2 back rashers bacon

2 tbsp corn oil

Skin the rabbits and remove the heads, if not already done for you! With kitchen scissors, cut away the bone and as much of the ribcage as possible. You should be left with 8 pieces of rabbit. Place in a large bowl.

To make the marinade, simply combine the ingredients, season with black pepper, and mix well. Pour over the rabbit, which must be turned in the marinade as often as possible, and leave for at least 12 hours, covered in the refrigerator.

For the potatoes, choose baby ones, and leave their skins on. I like to boil them first for 5 minutes in a pan of salted boiling water. Drain and allow to cool. This pre-cooking enables everything to be cooked together.

Remove the rabbit from its marinade, and coat the pieces with the breadcrumb, garlic and flour mixture, then arrange on a baking tray. Place the potatoes in a roasting dish. Chop the bacon rashers into small pieces and sprinkle over the potatoes, followed by the oil.

Place the baking tray and roasting dish in a preheated oven at 200°C/400°F/Gas 6 for 30 minutes. Remove both from the oven, and arrange on a serving plate. The rabbit should be crunchy on the outside and succulent on the inside. Serve with boiled baby carrots and garden peas. You will find it was well worth the effort.

Venison Steak with Sweetened Berries

*T*he smell of this winter dish always reminds me of Christmas. I use local venison, but I don't have it hung for too long as it gets far too gamey. Venison has become much more generally available than it used to be, and using prime cuts means that you can cook it more easily and simply than in the traditional roasting or stewing recipes.

Serves 4

4 × 6 oz (175 g) venison
    leg steaks
1 tbsp corn oil

SWEETENED BERRIES
4 oz (110 g) mixed
    berries (cranberries,
    redcurrants,
    blackberries,
    gooseberries)
1 tbsp olive oil
2 oz (55 g) sugar
2 tsp lemon juice
1 cinnamon stick
4 cloves
¼ pint (150 ml) red
    wine

Heat the corn oil in a frying pan, then fry the steaks for 2 minutes on both sides. Remove the pan from the heat and the steaks from the pan. Place the steaks in a hot oven preheated to 200°C/400°F/Gas 6 for 8–10 minutes.

During this time, gently soften the fruit in a saucepan with the olive oil and the juices from the steaks, about 2–3 minutes. Add the remaining ingredients, bring back to the boil, and simmer for a further 2–3 minutes.

Arrange the steaks on hot plates, and spoon the fruity sauce over (first removing the whole spices). Serve with baked potatoes and a crisp green salad.

Venison Sausages

*S*ausages were traditionally made with pork, a way of using up the very fatty cuts. The meat was put twice through the mincer, then water, cereal and seasonings were added. The mixture was then forced into the sausage skins, twisted and tied. Needless to say, after they were hung to dry overnight, they were eaten for breakfast.

Making sausages at home is not as complicated as one might think, and can be achieved with fairly basic equipment. I make these venison sausages in my (virtually domestic) kitchen at The Old Coach House, and I serve them as a starter on the dinner menu.

Serves 4

1 × 2 lb (900 g) leg of
   venison
8 oz (225 g) pork
   belly fat
8 oz (225 g)
   breadcrumbs
1 tsp each of dried
   rosemary, mint
   and thyme
½ tsp each of salt and
   black pepper
4 fl oz (120 ml) chicken
   stock
sausage casing, soaked
   in cold water

Trim the venison and place in the freezer or ice compartment of the fridge. This chills the meat and makes it easy to cut with a sharp knife into very small pieces. Place the meat pieces in a grinder or food processor and process well. Repeat with the pork belly fat. Place the ground meats in a large mixing bowl, and add the remaining ingredients apart from the sausage casing. Mix with your hands or a spoon until the herbs, meat and fat have an even consistency.

Place the mixture into a sausage machine and force into the sausage casing. If you do not have a machine, or your local butcher is not willing to let you use his, you can use a piping bag to pipe the mixture into the sausage casing. Divide into 6 in (15 cm) sausages by twisting the casing. Leave to hang in a cool place overnight.

To cook, simply fry for 3–4 minutes in a little corn oil. I serve the sausages on a purée of peaches (simply peach flesh puréed with a little lemon juice) with a dollop of home-made chutney (see page 33) as you can see in the photograph on pages 8–9. Crusty bread is a good accompaniment as well.

Woodcock with Blackberry Juice

*G*ame has always been popular in Ireland, and particularly in Wicklow. Woodcock is known as king of the game birds. Its scurried flight enables only the keenest shot to bag it, so, needless to say, one doesn't come across woodcock very often. (But they can be found fresh in supermarkets and good butchers in the season.) Traditionally they are roasted, complete with head and intestines then, when cooked, they are split in half (including the head). The intestines are removed, spread on a piece of toast, and the two half birds are served on top of this again. The brains are often eaten as well. This doesn't appeal to me . . .

Quail could be cooked in much the same way.

Heat the olive oil in an ovenproof heavy-bottomed pan (a cast-iron skillet is perfect). Add the diced back rasher and cook until crisp. Remove from the hot oil and set aside. Now carefully place the bird or birds in the hot oil and turn several times for about 3 minutes. Place the hot pan in the oven preheated to 220°C/425°F/Gas 7 and cook for 8 minutes.

Meanwhile, in a small pan, boil the blackberries with the sugar, wine and lemon juice, about 4 minutes. Remove from the heat and strain through a fine sieve. Discard the berries.

Place the heel of bread in the oven, as you remove the bird from the oven and pan. Divide the bird in half and discard the intestines and head. The bird should still be pink and very succulent. Remove the bread heel from the oven; it should be crisp. Place the bread on a serving plate and pour over the sweetened blackberry juice. Arrange the bird on top of this, and garnish with parsley and diced bacon. Sprinkle with salt and pepper and enjoy.

Per person

1 woodcock (available
   frozen, as you may
   wait for a fresh one!)
2 tbsp olive oil
1 back rasher bacon
   (not smoked), diced
   as finely as you can
1 heel (the end piece)
   sliced bread
chopped parsley
salt and pepper

BLACKBERRIES

1 oz (25 g) blackberries,
   fresh or frozen
1 tsp dark brown sugar
2 tbsp dry wine (red or
   white)
1 tsp lemon juice

Fraughan Pie

The first Sunday in August used to be the traditional day for picking these fraughan (Old Irish) or frockan (current usage), which are wild bilberries or blueberries. Not everybody will have the time (or the number of children necessary) to collect them, but most supermarkets will have cultivated blueberries when in season (July to August). Blueberries are much bigger and a lot sweeter than the wild fraughan.

For this recipe you will need shortcrust pastry, and I give a recipe, but frozen pastry will suffice.

Serves 4

PASTRY

4 oz (110 g) plain flour

a pinch of salt

2 oz (55 g) Irish butter
 or margarine

1–2 tbsp cold water

FILLING

1 lb (450 g) fraughans
 or blueberries

4 oz (110 g) light brown
 or cane sugar

2 tbsp clear honey

juice of 2 large lemons
 or 2 fl oz (55 ml)
 lemon juice

TO FINISH

1 egg, beaten

caster sugar

To make the pastry, sieve the flour and salt together into a bowl, then rub in the butter until a breadcrumb consistency. Gradually add enough water to bind the ingredients. Divide the pastry in two and roll out on a lightly floured pastry board to about ⅛ in (3 mm) thick. Place one sheet of the pastry on a greased 10 in (25 cm) ovenproof pie plate, and prick with a fork. Bake blind for about 10 minutes in a hot oven preheated to 200°C/400°F/Gas 6. When cooked, allow to cool, while you proceed with the filling.

In a mixing bowl combine all the filling ingredients and pour on top of the cooked pastry. Cover the entire plate with the second sheet of pastry, and press the edges together. Trim the edges, then prick the entire top with a fork, and paint with beaten egg. Place in the oven, still at the same temperature, for 20 minutes or until golden brown.

When cooked, sprinkle with caster sugar and serve with whipped cream or your favourite ice cream.

Orange Marmalade with Heather Flowers

The Wicklow Mountains glow purple because of the native heather. This provides a snack for the mountain sheep, as well as a habitat for the rabbits, and it was also said to give good luck to the traveller. The purple flowers are very bitter and even the sheep will not graze on them for very long. As a child I used to add them to lemonade to make it even more bitter, and gave it to my 'favourite' cousins.

To add this bitterness to a marmalade, collect a handful of heather flowers and have a piece of muslin handy to make into a bag.

Remove the juice and pips from the oranges and lemons. Put the juice into a large pot and put the pips with the heather flowers in the piece of muslin. Tie up into a bag and place in with the juice. Slice the orange skin into thick pieces and place in the pot with the juice. Add the water and bring to the boil. Reduce the heat and simmer for 1½–2 hours or until the orange skin is soft and breaks up easily. Remove the muslin parcel and leave it to cool.

Add the sugar to the liquid, heat gently to melt it thoroughly, then bring to a hard boil. Boil on for 15–20 minutes. Squeeze the cooled muslin bag over the pan to get out all the final juices.

Testing should be done after 15 minutes. If you have not made jam or marmalade before, it is best to use a sugar thermometer to ensure a good set, as over-boiling causes darkening of the preserve and a poor set. Setting point is 104°C (220°F). Or you can put teaspoonfuls on chilled saucers; if the marmalade has a very crinkly skin when you push it with your finger, setting point has been reached. If not, carry on boiling and testing (but do not *over*-boil).

Remove the marmalade from the heat and allow to cool slightly. Pour into prepared clean and warm jars, wipe clean, then seal, label and store.

I never gave this marmalade to the cousins as they had got quite fond of the very bitter lemonade . . .

Makes about 10 lb (4.5 kg)

3 lb (1.4 kg) any type of oranges
2 lemons
a handful of heather flowers
6 pints (3.4 litres) water
6 lb (2.75 kg) sugar

from the
VALLEYS

Between the mountains and hills lie the lush wooded river valleys in which a majority of the Wicklow population lives. In these fertile valley plains the 'Garden of Ireland' can truly be seen at its best. Corn, wheat and barley ripen in long fields along the riverbanks, and it is here that you can find many hares and rabbits sharing in the plenty. In domestic gardens, vegetable plots and small organic farms, potatoes, apples, peas and tomatoes are grown, with slightly more exotic produce occasionally seen.

Potatoes are linked in everyone's minds with Ireland, and they are said to have been introduced by Sir Walter Raleigh and first grown in the West at his estate in Youghal, County Cork, not too far from Wicklow. The potato blight that struck Ireland in the late 1840s – by then virtually a one-crop country – led to the tragedy of the Irish potato famine, and to a million deaths

and two million people emigrating to all parts of the globe. Even today, almost every house in the valleys will have a row or two of potatoes, the most popular varieties being those that are dry, not waxy, and which have to be boiled in their skins because otherwise they would dissolve into a pot of soup. Colcannon is one of the most famous Irish potato dishes, along with champ and boxty; I have added another couple of potato dishes from my childhood, and there are quite a few potato recipes elsewhere throughout the book – my homage to the Irish potato!

There's a nice little Wicklow rhyme which gently mocks the people of Cork:

Are you from Cork? / I am-aroo.
Do you eat potatoes? / Bedad I do.
How do you eat them? / Skins and all.
Do they not choke you? / Sure, not at all!

The notion of the potato's huge popularity in Ireland was gently mocked in an episode of *Ballykissangel* when Kathleen Hendley, owner of the general store, was asked to take part in a promotional film. She was supposed to tell the camera that potato bread was the most popular item she sold. But Kathleen refused to say that. Her best selling line, she insisted, was Pot Noodle . . .

Many houses and farms also have a small orchard, often perhaps a tree or two only, of cooking apples or small dessert apples. These are used in any number of ways, and the windfalls are never wasted – if we can get to them before the squirrels, blackbirds, rabbits, hares, pheasants . . .

Colcannon

This traditional Irish potato dish was served on Hallowe'en, and it would often contain four symbols – a gold band for marriage, a sixpence for wealth, a thimble to signify spinsterhood, and a button for bachelorhood. When we were children, my sister didn't much like colcannon, so my mother used to wrap a lot of loose change in greaseproof paper and put that in the dish to ensure its consumption. A clever move!

Kale is traditionally used in many parts of Ireland, but white or Savoy cabbage can be substituted. On our east coast, parsnip is sometimes added. You can see my colcannon in the photograph on page 91, alongside another traditional Irish dish, bacon with cabbage.

Serves 4

1½ lb (675 g) potatoes
8 oz (225 g) kale
1 medium leek
¼ pint (150 ml) milk
  and top of the milk
  (or single cream)
a pinch of mace
salt and pepper
4 oz (110 g) Irish butter

Peel, wash and thinly slice the potatoes. Cover with cold water and bring to the boil, reduce the heat and simmer until soft. Remove the stalks from the kale and chop the leaves into strips of about 1 in (2.5 cm). Slice the leek.

After simmering the potato for 10 minutes, add the chopped kale and sliced leek, then bring back to the boil and simmer for a further 10 minutes. Remove from the heat and drain away the liquid (the lid is better than a sieve for this). Do not mash, but to get the exact consistency, add the milk and top of milk and whisk until the potatoes are creamy. Season with mace, salt and pepper.

My mother used to form a volcano shape with the hot colcannon, and place the butter in the middle of the crater where it would melt. My children play the same games with it now as we did – and as they obviously did years ago, as recorded in this rhyme about colcannon:

> Did you ever scoop a hole on top
> To hold the melting lake
> Of the clover-coloured butter
> Which your mother used to make?

Stuffed Potatoes and Baked Tomatoes

*W*hen I was a child we used to make this for our Saturday lunch. It's very easy.

Peel, wash and dry the potatoes. Using an apple corer, make 4–6 holes in each potato. Place the sausagemeat in a piping bag and pipe into each cavity. Repeat this until all the potatoes are prepared, and then place them on a baking sheet and into the preheated oven at 200°C/400°F/ Gas 6 for 50 minutes. Turn the potatoes once after 25 minutes.

About 10 minutes before the potatoes will be ready, sprinkle grated cheese over them. Add the tomatoes to the baking sheet – butterfly them first, cutting them in two but not quite through, dredging them in olive oil and sprinkling with sea salt. Bake on for 10 minutes. Serve on a bed of lettuce and garnish with bacon pieces if you like.

Serves 4

8 medium potatoes

1 lb (450 g)
   sausagemeat

2 oz (55 g) firm Irish
   (Cheddar) cheese,
   grated

8 tomatoes

olive oil

sea salt

New Season Potatoes

*O*n the first Sunday in June my mother would dig up a quarter row of potatoes. They were small, waxy and very dirty. They would be brought down to the beach and washed in the wet sand first, and then in the sea. They were put in a large cauldron and covered with sea water and a handful of sea salt. The cauldron was placed in the middle of a driftwood fire and boiled until all the water had boiled away. The cauldron was removed from the fire, and butter and chopped cooked bacon were stirred in. The aroma would send us running up the beach. You can achieve something very similar at home.

Serves 4

2 lb (900 g) small new
  potatoes
8 back rashers bacon,
  finely chopped
2 oz (55 g) Irish butter
sea salt

Thoroughly wash the new potatoes and instead of boiling them, steam over boiling water. Gently fry the bacon in the butter until just cooked. Combine the ingredients in a mixing bowl and sprinkle with sea salt to taste. Serve in a bowl and eat outside in the garden.

Windfall Soup

*M*ost Wicklow people would have apples and other orchard fruits, and you're always trying to use them up in some way. This soup was traditionally made in August, using the windfalls from the apple trees. Being unripe, the apples had a considerable sharpness to them!

Collect the windfalls and remove any bruises. Do not peel. Wash in salted water and cover with cold water until ready for use.

Melt the butter in a suitable pan and gently heat the onion and garlic until the onion is starting to cook. Add the carrot, stir and gently simmer until the carrot changes colour. Add the stock and bring to the boil. Simmer for 5 minutes.

Remove the windfalls from the water and grate them directly into the simmering soup. Simmer for a further 5 minutes. Season with salt and pepper. Spoon into hot soup bowls, and a nice garnish is a sprig of freshly plucked lemon balm.

Serves 4

1 lb (450 g) windfall
  apples
salt and pepper
½ oz (15 g) Irish butter
1 medium onion, peeled
  and finely chopped
1 garlic clove, peeled
  and finely chopped
1 lb (450 g) carrots,
  scrubbed and grated
3 pints (1.8 litres)
  chicken stock

Cucumber and Apple Soup

This is a summer soup, which can be served hot or cold, and is a good way of using up oddly shaped cucumbers (as well as extra apples). My father used to sell his home-grown cucumbers to the local hotel, which of course only wanted to take the ones that were almost straight. As most cucumbers in those days were naturally curled, we ended up with the bulk of the crop at home (see also the chutney on page 33).

Serves 4

1 medium onion, peeled

1 garlic clove, peeled

½ oz (15 g) Irish butter

2 large cucumbers

2 eating apples, cored

1½ pints (900 ml)
   chicken stock

salt and pepper

Roughly chop the onion and garlic and gently fry in the butter in a suitable pot. Peel and slice the cucumbers and apples and place in the pot. Cover with the chicken stock and bring to the boil. Reduce the heat and simmer for 5 minutes. Blend the soup with a hand blender or in a food processor. Season with salt and pepper.

Serve hot with garlic bread, garnished with chives and a little cream. Alternatively, chill the soup in the fridge, and garnish it with cucumber slices and a little natural yoghurt. My sisters used to love it this way, but I must admit to always having had this thing about cold soup . . .

Buttered Hare with Rosemary and Tarragon Sauce

The hare is native to Ireland (as rabbit is not), and folklore claims that hares sucked milk from dairy cows during the night (along with hedgehogs, apparently). I have here allied the flesh of hare with another dairy product.

The traditional way of cooking hare is to casserole it with red wine, which leaves you with a gravy dish. Very flavourful, but the meat could be chicken, venison, beef, rabbit – or even hare. The taste is of the wine, so for this dish, why not have the wine in a glass!

Jowl bacon – from the cheek, obviously – is normally waste product, so ask your butcher to save you some. It's very fatty and very cheap.

Skin and clean both hares, if not already done for you. Remove the back bones and ribcages and discard. You will be left with 3 pieces of meat per person. Pierce holes through the meat and fill each hole with a little butter until half the butter is used up. Wrap a piece of jowl bacon around each piece of buttered meat and refrigerate for 2–3 hours or overnight.

In a small pan melt some of the remaining butter, and cook the chopped garlic for a few minutes, then add the remaining butter and melt. Place the hare pieces in a suitable baking dish. Pour the melted garlic butter over the hare, cover the baking dish with foil, and place in the preheated oven at 180°C/350°F/Gas 4 for 40 minutes. Remove from the oven.

To make the sauce, take 4 tbsp of melted butter from the baking dish and place in a small pan. Add the cream, rosemary, tarragon and black pepper, and bring to the boil. Simmer for about 2–3 minutes until it starts to thicken.

Remove the jowl bacon (which you don't serve), and arrange the hare pieces on a serving plate. Spoon the sauce over – just a little. Serve with baked potatoes, a crisp green salad and, of course, a glass of wine.

Serves 4

2 young hares
8 oz (225 g) Irish butter (unsalted is best)
4 oz (110 g) jowl bacon, thinly sliced (you need 12 rashers)
2 garlic cloves, peeled and crushed
¼ pint (150 ml) single cream
4 sprigs rosemary
2 sprigs tarragon
black pepper

Stuffed Baked Apples

When I was a boy, I used to 'box the fox', the Irish phrase for scrumping. We would then heat our prizes on a primus stove, but just to add taste rather than actually cook them. Delicious! Pick medium-sized cooking apples for this dish. Prick the skins with a fork as you would baking potatoes, to prevent the apples from exploding.

Serves 4

4 cooking apples

2 oz (55 g) sultanas

2 oz (55 g) dark brown
   sugar

4 tbsp honey

icing sugar

Clean and prick the apples (see above). With an apple corer or small sharp knife remove the cores from the apples. Mix the sultanas and sugar and press into the cavity of each apple, being careful not to crack the apple open. Place each apple in a separate ovenproof bowl. Pour 1 tbsp of the honey over each apple. Place the bowls in the preheated oven at 180°C/350°F/Gas 4 for 10–12 minutes. Remove from the oven, sprinkle with icing sugar, and serve with whipped cream or ice cream.

Apple and Plum Suet Pudding

Steamed suet puddings have been known and loved in Ireland for centuries. Traditionally they would have been simmered for hours on a kitchen fire or coal-burning stove on winter days. Nowadays a modern steamer may be used, or you can stand the basin on an old saucer in a saucepan of boiling water. Any fruit may be cooked in this recipe: we used plums in the photograph on page 20, but you could try gooseberries or rhubarb.

Butter a 1¾ pint (1 litre) pudding basin.

Peel the apples and chop them and the plums roughly. Put 1½ oz (40 g) of each aside for the topping. Mix the remaining fruit in a large bowl with the suet, breadcrumbs, 4 oz (110 g) of the sugar, nutmeg and salt. Add the beaten eggs and enough milk to get a dropping consistency. Leave to stand for 1 hour.

Test the mixture by stirring: if it feels stiff, add a little more milk. Pour the mixture into the prepared basin and cover with greased greaseproof paper or foil – with a pleat in to allow for expansion – and secure tightly with string. Place the pudding basin into the perforated part of a steamer or stand it on an old saucer in the saucepan. If you are boiling the pudding, the water should come halfway up the sides of the basin. Cover the pan tightly and steam the pudding over gently simmering water for 1¾–2 hours. Meanwhile, stew the retained fruit with the remaining sugar and 1 oz (25 g) butter until softened.

Serve the pudding from the bowl or turn out, after allowing to stand for about 10 minutes, on to a serving plate. Serve with the fruit topping and home-made custard (see overleaf) or whipped cream.

Serves 4

Irish butter

4½ oz (160 g) cooking apples

4½ oz (160 g) stoned plums

4 oz (110 g) shredded suet

4 oz (110 g) stale white breadcrumbs

5 oz (150 g) light brown sugar

¼ tsp grated nutmeg

a pinch of salt

2 eggs, beaten

about 4 fl oz (120 ml) milk

Vanilla Custard

*F*resh milk and free-range eggs are always available in Ballykissangel *country, and a custard made from them is second to none. Serve it with steamed or baked puddings, pies, tarts and stewed fruits.*

Serves 4

17 fl oz (500 ml) milk

½ tsp vanilla essence

6 egg yolks

4 oz (110 g) caster sugar

2 tsp cornflour

Place the milk and vanilla essence into a small saucepan and heat gently. Do not let it boil.

Meanwhile beat the egg yolks, sugar and cornflour together in a bowl until creamy. Add the warm milk, then strain the mixture back into the pan. Cook, stirring constantly, until the custard thickens and coats the back of the spoon.

This may be served hot or cold.

Cucumber Chutney

We would usually make a lot of this chutney, another way of using up my father's unwanted cucumbers. I serve it with sausages, as photographed on pages 8–9.

Cut a 6 in (15 cm) square out of muslin and place on a flat surface. Put the pickling spices in the centre and tie one corner diagonally with the opposite corner. Do the same with the other corners, so that you have a secure parcel. Place this in a suitably large preserving pan.

Chop the cucumbers, cooking apples, peeled onions, garlic and dried apricots, and place in the pot. Add the sultanas, raisins, cloves, mustard seeds, black peppercorns and salt, and cover with malt vinegar. Bring to the boil and simmer for 1 hour. Remove the pickling spices from the chutney and discard.

Seed the chillies, discarding the seeds, and cut the flesh into strips. Add with the sugar to the chutney and return gently to the boil, allowing the sugar to melt first. Reduce the heat and simmer for a further 30–40 minutes – or longer if necessary – until the mixture is jam consistency.

Spoon the chutney into prepared clean and warm jars – you'll need about seven 1 lb (450 g) jars. Seal with vinegar-proof covers, then leave to cool. Wrap each jar in brown paper and store in a cool dark place to mature. Finished off with a pretty top and label, the jars of chutney make great Christmas gifts.

3 lb (1.4 kg) cucumbers
3 lb (1.4 kg) cooking
  apples, cored
8 oz (225 g) onions
3 garlic cloves, peeled
4 oz (110 g) each of
  dried apricots,
  sultanas and raisins
6 cloves
2 oz (55 g) yellow
  mustard seeds
1 tbsp black peppercorns
1 tbsp salt
1½ pints (900 ml) clear
  malt vinegar
6 fresh red chillies
4 lb (1.8 kg) sugar

PICKLING SPICES

6 bay leaves
1 cinnamon stick
3 nutmegs
6 cloves
2 oz (55 g) dried chillies
1 tbsp allspice berries
1 piece mace
2 oz (55 g) dried ginger

from the
RIVERS

Wicklow is studded with streams and boasts many fine rivers, which flow down from the mountains into the Irish Sea. Not too far from The Old Coach House and the village of Avoca is The Meeting of the Waters, where the rivers Avonmore and Avonbeg come together to form the Avoca river; there is a little memorial garden there, and the stark remnants of the tree under which Thomas Moore is said to have composed his famous song.

'There is not in this wide world a valley so sweet
As the vale in whose bosom the bright waters meet.
Oh! The last rays of feeling and life must depart
Ere the bloom of that valley shall fade from my heart.'

The rivers are teeming with life. Fish include freshwater varieties such as pike, perch, tench and trout, and then of course there are the migrants, the salmon and eel, which travel from virtually the other side of the world to come back to their native Irish waters. (There are even salmon in the Liffey, but they come in up a tributary, not through the port of Dublin.) Salmon fishing is one of the prime sports in Ireland, but salmon poaching is just as famous, particularly so in Wicklow. They use nets, all highly illegal, and rivers have been known to get so low that the poachers can just pluck the salmon out of the pools.

The most popular fish, however, is the little local brown trout. Its delicate flavour can really only be enjoyed at its best by gutting and cleaning in the river in which it was caught. Many is the time I've prepared for a fishing trip by taking along a primus stove, matches, frying pan, butter, salt and pepper and, oh yes, a rod. Once caught, the fish is simply fried in the butter. In *Ballykissangel*, schoolmaster Brendan Kearney regularly fishes the river Angel for its succulent little trout.

There are a number of farmed trout in the rivers in Wicklow, for when the rivers fill after heavy rain, the trout farms overflow and many fish escape. They're easy to catch on bait because they're so used to being fed!

The other bounty of the rivers is wild duck, primarily mallard, teal and widgeon, and they have been eaten and enjoyed for centuries.

Another 'product' of the Avoca rivers is gold, and there was a considerable gold rush in the late eighteenth century. After Liam and Donal were searching for gold in one of the *Ballykissangel* episodes, a second mini gold rush looked imminent!

Pike Baked in Newspaper

This predator is at the top of the fish food chain, and its only rival would be bigger pike and, of course, skilled fishermen! Unless you fish yourself you will have to order pike, as they are not readily available, but they certainly provide a very interesting talking point on a buffet table, an alternative to a poached salmon with mayonnaise (still the most popular dish to serve at an Irish wedding).

You will need four pages of newspaper – **The Sunday** or **Irish Times** is good.

Serves about 12

1 large pike, about 10 lb
   (4.5 kg) in weight
3 or 4 large potatoes,
   peeled
2 heads lollo rosso
2 heads curly endive
about 20 small
   tomatoes
mayonnaise
2 oz (55g) clarified
   butter
fresh dill, chopped

Clean the pike and pat it dry with kitchen paper. Place the whole potatoes inside the pike so it can rest on them and keep its shape. (Potatoes are also used in Ireland to keep a roasting goose in shape, and absorb all those wonderful flavours.) Place the fish on newspaper, fold the sides in and fold over three or four times, depending on the size of the fish. Place on a baking tray and bake in the oven preheated to 180°C/350°F/Gas 4 for 35–40 minutes. Test with a skewer – if it goes through without any resistance, it's ready – and remove from the oven. Carefully unroll the newspaper, and you will find the skin will stick to the paper, leaving you with a perfect fish. Allow to become cold.

Arrange the lettuce leaves alternately around a large serving plate and place the fish in the centre. Arrange the tomatoes randomly around the fish. Put the mayonnaise in a piping bag and pipe with either a rose or star nozzle completely around the base of the fish. Heat the clarified butter and paint over the entire fish, using a pastry brush. Sprinkle with chopped dill, and prepare yourself for loads of admiration.

Steamed Perch with Lemon and Cream Sauce

*T*his freshwater fish was not eaten traditionally, but was mainly used as bait to catch bigger fish like pike. I think it was the size that was the reason because they were usually small and rather bony. Today, however, perch have been allowed to mature and the size has increased a little, so you will need at least two fish per person. The tasty white flesh has a wonderful sweetness, but filleting is highly recommended.

If you can't find perch, any small fish fillets can be cooked in this way.

Place the perch fillets in a steamer, and steam for 3–4 minutes.

Melt the butter in a small pan, add the cream and bring to the boil. Simmer until the cream has reduced by one-third. Remove from the heat and add the lemon juice, and salt and pepper to taste. Return to the heat and simmer gently.

Arrange the perch fillets on a serving dish, and pour the sauce over them. Sprinkle with parsley and garnish with lemon wedges. Served with toasted brown bread, it's perfect!

Serves 4

1¼–1½ lb (550–675 g)
   perch fillets
1 oz (25 g) Irish butter
¼ pint (150 ml) single
   cream
1 tbsp lemon juice
salt and pepper
parsley and lemon
   wedges to garnish

Marinated Trout with Mustard and Dill

*I*n 1996 they held the All Ireland fishing competition in Avoca, and they stocked the river from The Meetings through Avondale up to Rathdrum with specimen fish of about 5 lb (2.25 kg). In the ten days of the competition, the largest fish caught was about 10 oz (275 g), so, in theory, the large fish are there still . . .

This will make a delightful change for a summer lunch. It is a simple dish, but you need to prepare it the night before.

Serves 4

4 whole trout
salt and pepper
juice of 1 lemon
¼ pint (150 ml) dry
    white wine
2 tbsp grain mustard
4 sprigs fresh dill, finely
    chopped

Bone and skin the trout, then clean and dry the 8 fillets with kitchen paper. Place in a suitable dish in one layer, and season with salt and pepper. Mix the lemon juice, wine, mustard and dill, ensuring a good blend. Pour over the fish fillets, cover with a plate and refrigerate overnight. If at all possible, turn the fish in the marinade as often as you can.

Before serving, remove the fillets from the marinade and slice lengthways into pieces ⅛ in (3 mm) thick. Serve with baby new potatoes, sliced tomatoes and cucumber, and a generous amount of mayonnaise.

Stuffed Baked Salmon with Green Sauce

My grandfather was the first Irishman to drive a tram, as all the original drivers came over from England. When he retired, he became a gardener. My main memories of him are his pipe, which smoked like a train, his big old coat which I couldn't even lift, and his habit of walking very fast, so fast that I had to run to keep up with him.

This recipe comes from my grandfather, whose green sauce for salmon was made with nettles. He loved the taste of nettles and used them in everything he could (they're famous as a blood purifier, particularly good for the skin, in Irish folklore). You will need only a few young leaves. Sorrel, spinach or dandelion leaves could be substituted for the nettles.

Have the fishmonger bone the steaks, but leave the skin on. Peel the onion, and then roughly chop the onion and walnuts. Mix the breadcrumbs, onion, walnuts, salt, pepper and egg until a ball is formed. Divide the mixture into four, and place a piece inside the 'hole' in each salmon steak.

In an ovenproof frying pan or skillet heat the butter and quickly seal both sides of each steak. Place in the oven preheated to 180°C/350°F/Gas 4 for 15 minutes.

For the sauce, roughly chop the nettle leaves and the chive stalks. Heat the butter in a small pan, then add the cornflour and stir until it forms a smooth paste. Remove from the heat, and add the chicken stock, cream, nettles and chives. Whisk until everything is combined, then return to the heat and bring to the boil, stirring all the time. The sauce should be smooth and creamy (if not, allow to simmer on until you achieve the desired result).

Remove the salmon steaks from the oven and arrange on a serving plate. Spoon the sauce over the steaks, and garnish with nasturtium flowers if you like.

Serves 4

4 × 5–6 oz (150–175 g) salmon steaks

1 small onion

3 shelled walnuts

2 oz (55 g) brown breadcrumbs

salt and pepper

1 egg, beaten

½ oz (15 g) Irish butter

SAUCE

8–10 nettle leaves

3–4 chive stalks

1 oz (25 g) Irish butter

1 tsp cornflour

¼ pint (150 ml) chicken stock

¼ pint (150 ml) single cream

Salmon in a Basket

*T*here are many salmon rivers in Ireland and Irish salmon is world famous. It's cooked in a number of ways, and we also smoke it. Smoked Irish salmon with scrambled eggs is a favourite breakfast at The Old Coach House.

Serves 4

4 × 4–6 oz (110–175 g)
  fillets of fresh wild
  Irish salmon, skinned
6 oz (175 g) puff pastry
4 oz (110 g) Irish butter
1 large leek, cleaned
  and finely sliced
salt and pepper
1 egg, beaten

Roll the pastry out into 4 separate squares that will comfortably enclose the fillets. Put one-quarter of the butter in a knob in the centre of each square. Put one-quarter of the finely sliced leek on top of the butter, and a fillet of fish on top of that. Season with salt and pepper.

Egg wash the edges of the pastry, fold in and seal on top. Add pastry decorations if you like. Egg wash the top. Place the 'baskets' on a baking tray and into the preheated oven at 200°C/400°F/Gas 6 for 12–15 minutes, or until the pastry turns light brown.

Serve on a warmed plate with steamed vegetables – new potatoes and green beans in the photograph on page 34 – or a crisp salad.

Wild Duck with Game Chips

T he lakes and rivers of Wicklow are home to a range of wild ducks. The tradition of game hunting is as old as the gun (probably older), and although I never participate in the sport, I certainly enjoy the rewards.

Mallard are best hung for a day or two. They are then plucked and trussed, ready for cooking. They are simply roasted, and are usually served slightly underdone as they have a tendency to dry out. You could use domestic duck instead, fresh or frozen, but you'd have to cook it for longer.

Serves 4

2 mallard
2 oz (55 g) beef
    dripping or goose fat
salt and pepper
¼ pint (150 ml) port

GAME CHIPS
2–3 potatoes, peeled
    and very thinly sliced
corn oil for deep-frying

Prepare the mallard as described above. Place the dripping or goose fat in a roasting tray in a preheated oven at 200°C/400°F/Gas 6 until it has melted and is hot. Place the mallard in the hot dripping, baste, return to the oven and roast for 5 minutes. Remove from the oven again, season with salt and pepper, and carefully pour the port over each bird. Baste well, return to the oven, and roast for another 10 minutes, basting once more during this time. Remove from the oven and split each bird in half. Place on a serving plate and keep warm.

Serve with game chips, which are simply thin slices of potato deep-fried until golden brown (best done in small batches). Drain really well on kitchen paper. A light gravy can also be served but it is really not necessary as the succulent meat will provide its own juices.

Wild Duck Poached in Red Wine

*W*idgeon is somewhat similar in taste to mallard, but its skin has the most peculiar taste, and if you were to roast this duck in the conventional way you most certainly would not eat it. So you must cook the widgeon in the same fashion as pigeon, with the skin removed and, as a rule, breast meat removed from the breast bone.

Try to get birds from the rivers rather than the coast, as the sea variety can be a bit salty. Substitute Barbary duck breasts, if you like, but one only per person, and cook for double the time, about 4 minutes.

In a lidded frying pan gently brown your whole onions in the butter or oil, then add the celery, garlic, wine, peppercorns and bay leaf. Bring to the boil, and simmer for a few minutes. Place the widgeon breasts on top of the celery and onion, and cover the pan with its lid for 2 minutes. The meat cooks in the steam. Remove the bay leaf.

I like to serve this on a heel of bread dried in the oven, but a piece of lightly toasted bread will suffice. Place the widgeon fillets on the bread and cover with the vegetable and wine sauce.

Serves 4

8 widgeon breast fillets
8–10 silverskin (pickling) onions, peeled
½ oz (15 g) Irish butter or a little olive oil
2 celery sticks, finely chopped
2 garlic cloves, peeled and crushed
¼ pint (150 ml) red wine
6 black peppercorns
1 bay leaf
4 baked heels of bread or toast

from the
FIELDS AND
PASTURES

The pasture fields around *Ballykissangel* and all over Wicklow are the rich bright green so characteristic of Ireland. The soil is so fine, so uniquely fertile, that in one episode Brian Quigley planned to dig up an entire hillside and sell it off to gardeners living elsewhere. The lush grass, studded with wild flowers and herbs, feeds the cattle that produce Irish beef and the plump sheep that give a simple Irish stew such flavour. A side benefit of the animals' presence in the fields is the mass of field mushrooms that appear from July to September. If you're confident about identifying them properly, they make a wonderful breakfast, but only pick them in the morning as they quickly dissolve and turn black in the sun because of their high water content.

Beef used to be a meat for special occasions only. When a cow was slaughtered, it was usually preserved by pickling, corning or salting, so that it would last the winter – much more practical than eating the meat fresh. In the eighteenth century Cork used to be the principal centre for the corning industry, exporting corned beef all over Europe. Corned beef was traditionally served with cabbage and floury potatoes, and I give a recipe for that here, but I also cook it in Guinness, the famous black stout that has been made in Dublin since 1759.

Nothing was wasted from the beef either, and the many offal recipes that exist in Cork and Wicklow reflect the fact that while the prime pieces of meat may have been sent abroad, the offal stayed at home.

Irish stew is one of the oldest and most famous of Irish recipes. It originated in the peasants' cabins where a pot over an open fire would be virtually the only means of cooking. The griskin, spare ribs, or scrag end of neck of mutton would be boiled with onions, potatoes and water. A nutritious and tasty one-pot meal, the liquid would often be served as a soup.

Corned (Pickled) Beef and Cabbage

My grandfather used to pickle his own beef. He used silverside or brisket, and his recipe for the brine was 5 pints water, 1 lb sea salt, 5 oz brown sugar, 2 tsp saltpetre, 2 tbsp mustard seeds, 1 tsp whole cloves, 2 tbsp black peppercorns, 1 tsp allspice and 6 bay leaves! This mixture was simmered for 30 minutes and allowed to go cold. The meat would be rubbed in salt and soaked in the brine for 3 days before being salted again and soaked for a further 4 days. The day before the meat was to be cooked, it would be steeped in cold water.

Nowadays corned beef can be bought at many a butcher.

Serves 4

2 lb (900 g) corned brisket or silverside, soaked for 12–24 hours
1 tsp dry mustard powder
1 large carrot
1 large onion, peeled
1 sprig each of parsley and thyme
4 whole cloves
1 large cabbage

Place the corned beef in a large saucepan, cover with cold water, add the mustard, and bring to the boil. Remove any scum. Add the carrot, onion, parsley, thyme and cloves. Bring back to the boil, reduce the heat and simmer for 50 minutes.

Cut the cabbage in quarters and place in the saucepan with the beef. Bring back to the boil and simmer, covered, for 30 minutes. Remove the beef from the liquid and slice. Arrange on a plate with the cabbage and serve with boiled potatoes.

Boxteen

This was a leftover dish, often served on a Monday, perhaps with a sausage or bacon rasher.

The liquid from cooking the corned beef was kept, and any vegetables available – potatoes, turnips etc. – would be boiled up in it and then mashed. It looked a bit like a porridge and wasn't very appealing, but if you were hungry you would eat it, and it had a good taste.

Corned Beef
in Guinness

This recipe is a variation on the classic dish opposite. You can serve it with the dumplings on page 53, cooking them in the hot liquid while the meat rests.

Serves 4

2 lb (900 g) corned
   brisket or silverside,
   soaked for 12–24
   hours
1 celery stick
1 large carrot
1 large onion, peeled
1½ pints (900 ml)
   Guinness
1 tsp dry mustard
   powder
1 tbsp chopped parsley
1 sprig thyme
2 bay leaves

Place the corned beef in a large pot. Slice the celery, carrot and onion, and add to the pot. Pour in the Guinness, adding water if there is not enough Guinness to cover the meat. Add the mustard, parsley, thyme and bay leaves. Bring to the boil and simmer, covered, for 1½ hours. Drain well.

Slice the meat and arrange on a serving plate. Serve with boiled cabbage to keep it traditional.

Stuffed Fillet of Beef

M ost butchers in Wicklow are small family-run businesses, and the quality of beef they sell you is the same quality as the last piece of beef they sold you. This is good for the consumer as you know you will always get what you want. Needless to say, the best cut is the fillet.

This is a foolproof method.

Serves 4

4 × 4–6 oz (110–175 g)
   fillet steaks

4 oz (110 g) fresh
   breadcrumbs

Irish butter

3 tbsp finely chopped
   parsley

4 back rashers bacon

Mix the breadcrumbs, 2 oz (55 g) of the butter and the parsley together; you will find they form a tight ball. Divide in four. Cut a 1 in (2.5 cm) slit in the side of each steak and force the stuffing into this. Wrap the back rasher around the stuffing and steak, then carefully press down on each steak until it is ¾ in (2 cm) thick.

Heat a little more butter in a frying pan and brown all sides of each steak for about 1 minute. Now the foolproof bit. Put the steaks into a preheated oven at 200°C/400°F/Gas 6 for 2 minutes for blue steak; 5 minutes for rare; 7 minutes for medium; and 10 minutes for well done. If you like charred beef, it is best to put it back on the pan and blacken it to your liking. Serve with garlic butter.

Oxtail Soup with Dumplings

Oxtails were left after the rest of the carcasses were corned and exported. (Pigs' tails are used in local recipes as well, but I'm not so keen on them.)

I remember an argument in school which concerned whether or not there were bones in oxtail soup. I insisted there were, and it all ended in a bloody nose for me and the realisation that I had never had oxtail soup made from a packet!

Fry the jointed oxtail in a dry soup pot until golden brown. Remove from the pot and fry the onion until it is transparent. Add the garlic and herbs and infuse with the onions. Add the water and replace the oxtail. Season with salt and pepper, bring to the boil, reduce the heat, and simmer for 2 hours. At this point remove from the heat and allow to cool. Remove surplus fat – which will have set in a layer across the pot – and top up with water if necessary. Mix the cornflour with a little water and add to the pot. Reheat to a simmer, stir well, and heat until you have a thickened but still liquid gravy.

For the dumplings, sieve the flour and mustard into a mixing bowl. Add the suet, salt and pepper and enough water to make a soft dough. Divide this mixture into 8 equal balls, then drop into the soup and cook for 10 minutes.

Carefully spoon the dumplings into a soup plate, followed by the oxtail and sauce. Serve with freshly made soda bread – and provide a knife and fork to those who don't know what to do with the bones!

Serves 4

1 oxtail, cut into pieces
2 onions, peeled and
    roughly chopped
2 garlic cloves, peeled
1 sprig each parsley and
    thyme
2 bay leaves
2½ pints (1.4 litres)
    water
salt and pepper
2 tbsp cornflour

DUMPLINGS

4 oz (110 g) self-raising
    flour
1 tsp dry mustard
    powder
2 oz (55 g) shredded
    suet
water to mix

Lying Tongue with Sherry Gravy

*M*y mother used to tell me that if you told lies, your tongue would be cut out of your head, cooked and end up in a sandwich for a good boy who **didn't** tell lies. Despite this, my favourite school sandwich was tongue, and I often wondered whose tongue it was!

Serves 4

1 ox tongue, weighing
   3½–4 lb (1.6–1.8 kg)
1 onion, peeled
2 garlic cloves, peeled
3 bay leaves
½ tsp salt
1 tsp black peppercorns

GRAVY
1½ oz (40 g) Irish
   butter
1½ oz (40 g) plain flour
¼ pint (150 ml) dry
   sherry
¼ pint (150 ml) chicken
   stock
2 tbsp redcurrant jelly
salt and pepper

Soak the tongue in cold water overnight, best done in the fridge. Drain and place in a suitable pot, cover with fresh cold water and bring to the boil. Boil for 5 minutes. Remove the tongue from the water and set aside. Discard the water and clean the pot. Replace the tongue in the cleaned pot and cover with fresh cold water yet again.

Roughly chop the onion and garlic and add to the liquid along with the bay leaves, salt and peppercorns. Bring to the boil, reduce the heat and gently simmer for 2½–3 hours, skimming the top of the water frequently.

Drain off the water then plunge the tongue into cold water. Remove from the cold water, peel the skin off and discard this. Slice the tongue diagonally into thick slices and keep warm.

For the gravy, melt the butter in a pan, stir in the flour, then gradually stir in the sherry and chicken stock. Bring to the boil, reduce the heat and simmer for 5 minutes. Add the redcurrant jelly with salt and pepper to taste, and simmer for a further minute. Pour over the sliced tongue.

Serve with potato cakes and garnish with sliced spring onions. The leftover tongue is ideal for sandwiches with a little mustard – and don't forget to warn your children!

Stuffed Flat Mushrooms with Shallots and Spinach

*I*f you don't pick your own, flat mushrooms can be found just about everywhere and all year round. They are sold as flat open caps and breakfast mushrooms, and they come in sizes ranging from 1 in (2.5 cm) diameter all the way up to 9 in (23 cm). I find 3 in (7.5 cm) ones are best suited to this succulent vegetarian dish, which you can see in the photograph on page 46.

Remove the stalks from the mushroom caps, and discard. Gently fry the shallot and garlic in the butter. Add the spinach to the pan and cook for a further 2 minutes. Remove from the heat and allow to cool.

Grate the cheeses into a bowl, then add the cold contents of the pan along with the cream, herbs, salt and pepper. Mix well.

Divide this mixture between the mushrooms on a baking tray, and bake in the preheated oven at 200°C/400°F/Gas 6 for 15 minutes.

I like to serve these mushrooms with baked potatoes or soda bread.

Per person

2–3 mushrooms

2 shallots, peeled and
    chopped

1 small garlic clove,
    peeled and crushed

½ oz (15 g) Irish butter

2 oz (55 g) fresh
    spinach, washed and
    chopped

½ oz (15 g) red
    Cheddar cheese

½ oz (15 g) mozzarella
    cheese

2 tbsp single cream

a pinch each of dried
    tarragon and oregano

salt and pepper

Rack of Wicklow Lamb with Rosemary Cream

A traditional Easter Sunday dinner would be of that season's kid, killed when very young. The meat would be so tender and tasty, you didn't need to do anything to it except add a few sprigs of rosemary. Two racks and two legs would feed four to six people. I have substituted some of our famous Wicklow lamb.

Serves 4

2 full racks of lamb

ROSEMARY CREAM
1 oz (25 g) Irish butter
2 sprigs fresh rosemary,
    about 6 in (15 cm)
    long
7 fl oz (200 ml) double
    cream
a pinch of salt

Trim the rib bones half way back to the eye, and then split each rack evenly in two, giving a 4–5 oz (110–150 g) piece per portion.

Sear the three sides of each piece of lamb in a dry pan, avoiding the bone. Place on a baking tray meat side down, bone side up, and roast in a preheated oven at 200°C/400°F/Gas 6, for 8 minutes.

Meanwhile make the rosemary cream. Melt the butter, then add the rosemary, cream and salt. Bring to the boil, and boil for barely 1 minute. Remove the rosemary. Place a generous spoonful of the cream on each warmed plate with the rack of lamb on top, meat side down with bones sticking up. Serve with lightly steamed carrots, puréed parsnip and roast potatoes.

Traditional Irish Stew

There is an expression in Ireland that comes from the sheep rustlers: 'Sure, you might as well be hung for a sheep as a lamb.' So, in other words, mutton was preferred, and the lamb was allowed to grow.

The other ingredients for Irish stew vary quite a lot from county to county, but I find the basic potato and onion by far the best – no carrot, no stock, no barley. In some recipes, only half the potatoes are sliced and layered, and the rest are laid whole on the top to steam over the meat. The sliced potatoes would thicken the liquid.

Separate the meat from the fat and bone. Fry the fat and the bones in a dry pan until you have a small amount of liquid fat. Discard the gristle and bones.

Arrange the meat, potato slices and chopped onion in layers in a casserole, seasoning each layer with salt and pepper. Place the herbs on top of the potato layer which you finish with. Pour the water into the frying pan with the small amount of fat, and mix. Pour this into the casserole. Place into the oven preheated to 150°C/300°F/Gas 2, and cook for 2 hours. The sauce should be creamy and the meat should be tender.

Serves 4

3 lb (1.4 kg) lamb (or mutton) neck chops
2 lb (900 g) potatoes, peeled and sliced
1 lb (450 g) onions, peeled and finely chopped
salt and pepper
2 sprigs thyme
4 sprigs parsley
1 pint (600 ml) water

from the
FORESTS

The dense forests that surround *Ballykissangel* are home to a huge variety of wild life – red squirrels, badgers, foxes, deer, birds such as tits – blue, great, long-tailed – and jays, magpies, hooded crows, pied and green woodpeckers, and birds of prey like sparrowhawks. There are also, of course, fungi, wild berries and the trees themselves. You can't see the wood for the trees, so they say, and oak, pine, hazel, beech, chestnut, willow, ash, poplar, sycamore and rowan all contribute to the forty shades of green.

The ever-changing leaf colours ensure that the forests never look the same, especially in autumn when the amber foliage provides the perfect habitat for the pheasant. Some of the gamekeepers in the forests breed pheasants, manў of which stroll down to the roads, so while driving, extra care must be taken for surely there will be a pheasant waiting around the next corner, ready to run out in front of you!

The forests are open to the public to remind us of what Ireland used to be like when it was covered by trees, and care must be taken not to disturb or damage them in any way. Countless outdoor scenes in *Ballykissangel* are set in or near these abundant woodlands. A tranquil stroll through the trees is a good way to get away from the stress and strain of everyday life, but watch out for the flies and a lot of midges in the morning and early evening!

I like to go walking in the forests in the morning, collecting puffball mushrooms or fruit from the hedgerows on the way. The flickering bright light through the green canopy illuminates the forest floor, pinpointing chanterelles, ceps, morels and parasols. Hazelnuts and sweet chestnuts are also collected, and in the evening when the light is not so bright, my friend the gamekeeper would be potting some wood pigeons. Later on, when the forest is dark, the eerie call of the fox can be heard, or is it the cry of the banshee of the woods?

Morels with Sherry and Cream

*F*resh morels are hard to come by, and expensive (although I have them in my garden and pick them in the forests). As they can be confused with false morels, seek out dried ones and reconstitute them by soaking in boiling water.

Serves 4

1 lb (450 g) fresh
  morels, or 6–8 oz
  (175–225 g) dried
  morels
8 shallots, peeled and
  chopped
3 oz (80 g) Irish butter
¼ pint (150 ml) dry
  sherry
½ pint (300 ml) single
  cream
1 sprig each of rosemary
  and thyme
salt and pepper
8 slices Soda Bread
  with Hazelnuts
  (see page 69)

Clean the fresh morels, and slice lengthways into 3 or 4 pieces. If using dried morels, soak for 20–30 minutes in about ½ pint (300 ml) boiling water to cover. Drain, but keep the water as it is now stock. (Strain the stock through a fine strainer to get rid of any sand or dirt.)

In a frying pan gently brown the shallot in the butter. Add the morels and the morel stock, bring to the boil and simmer for 10–12 minutes. Add the sherry and cream, rosemary and thyme, and a pinch each of salt and pepper. Bring back to the boil and simmer until the liquid has reduced by half and has become thick and creamy.

Meanwhile lightly toast the bread and arrange on a serving plate. (Toasting the bread brings out the nutty flavour, and is a good contrast to the unusual sweetness of the mushrooms.) Divide the morel mixture between the slices of toast, and serve immediately.

Forest Mushrooms with Sautéed Potatoes

Collecting forest or wild mushrooms is a skill, and should not be undertaken by the untrained as it could end in disaster. A wide variety can be purchased in your local supermarket or deli, fresh or dried. If using dried mushrooms, you must soak them in boiling water for 20–30 minutes. Then all you need to do is drain them, and you're ready to go.

Serves 4

1½ lb (675 g) fresh
    forest mushrooms, or
    12 oz (350 g) mixed
    dried
1½ lb (675 g) baby
    potatoes, scrubbed
2–3 tbsp olive oil
8 oz (225 g) silverskin
    (pickling) onions or
    shallots, peeled
1 garlic clove, peeled
    and crushed
2 oz (55 g) Irish butter
a pinch each of chopped
    parsley and thyme
salt and pepper
½ pint (300 ml) single
    cream

TO SERVE
½ head Cos lettuce
2 tbsp chopped parsley

If using fresh mushrooms, choose from ceps, chanterelles, oysters, shaggy caps or parasols. Wipe or brush clean. If using dried, soak as above, then drain.

Place the potatoes in a pot and cover with cold water. Bring to the boil and simmer for 10 minutes. Remove from the heat, drain and allow to cool. Cut the potatoes in half, and fry gently in the olive oil, turning often. Leave in the pan.

Using another pan, fry the whole onions and the crushed garlic in the butter until slightly browned, about 8 minutes. Remove the onions from the pan and keep warm.

Slice the fresh or soaked dried mushrooms and sauté them in the same pan as the onions and garlic, adding the thyme and parsley, and a pinch each of salt and pepper.

Empty the entire contents of the mushroom pan on top of the potatoes. Add the onions and finally all the cream. Increase the heat and bubble the liquid for 2–3 minutes until it starts to thicken.

Lastly, shred the Cos lettuce and divide between 4 serving plates. Dish the mushrooms and potatoes on top of the lettuce and garnish with parsley. This is one dish you will make over and over again.

Chicken Breast Stuffed with Chestnut

*W*hile collecting mushrooms in the forests you might want to collect sweet chestnuts. These do not grow to a large size, but they are well worth collecting for their taste. They must be ripened by placing them in a dry warm place for 7–10 days, during which time the shells will change colour and split open, revealing the nuts. They are cooked by boiling until tender, then the husks are removed. You are left with small sweet chestnuts, and lots of them!

If using wild chestnuts, follow the instructions as above. If using shop-bought chestnuts, boil for 10 minutes and remove the shells and husks. If using dried chestnuts, reconstitute by pouring boiling water over them and soaking for 30 minutes.

Chop or grate the nuts and mix with the breadcrumbs, lemon rind, lemon juice and butter. Divide the mixture into four. Cut one side of each chicken breast half-way through, and push a portion of stuffing into these pockets. Wrap a bacon rasher around each chicken breast.

Heat the oil in a pan, and fry each side of the chicken for 1 minute. Remove from the pan, place on a suitable plate and place in a steamer. Cover and steam for 10 minutes.

Serve with a crisp salad dressed with a nutty oil.

Serves 4

4 chicken breasts
4 back rashers bacon
1 tbsp corn oil

STUFFING

4 oz (110 g) chestnuts, cooked, or 2 oz (55 g) dried chestnuts
2 oz (55 g) fresh breadcrumbs
1 tsp grated lemon rind
juice of 1 lemon
1 oz (25 g) Irish butter

Pigeon Breast with Crispy Bacon

Pigeons are not bred for the table in Ireland, as there are quite enough of them already (although they used to be, judging by the pigeon lofts on a number of large houses). They are a nuisance to farmers and landowners, as they eat all the crops – thus my friend the gamekeeper's constant supply to The Old Coach House during the summer.

Traditionally pigeons were casseroled whole in a wine and beef stock, and had a tendency to be overcooked and overpowered by everything else in the casserole. They're also baked in a pie, but I prefer the breasts off the bone and simply cooked as here (and in the photograph on page 58).

Per person

2–3 pigeon breasts

1 back rasher bacon, diced

a little corn oil

1 tbsp red wine vinegar

a pile of lettuce leaves

chopped parsley

Dice the bacon and fry it in the oil in a pan until the pieces start to change colour. Remove and drain on kitchen paper.

Meanwhile, cut the pigeon breast meat away from the bone and butterfly it – slice it almost in two, then pat out to about ¼ in (5 mm) thickness.

Fry the meat in the hot bacon pan, turning only once. Add the red wine vinegar and boil. The total cooking time is about 2 minutes. The meat should be quite pink and very succulent.

Place the meat on top of the salad leaves, sprinkle with chopped bacon and parsley, and eat immediately.

Pheasant with Garlic Crumble and Coach House Potatoes

*O*ur local Avoca butcher, Isaac Lett, is the source of all information. I once asked him about
pheasant and he said he'd get me a few. Forty brace turned up, so fresh they were still
twitching. What a job that was, plucking and gutting them quickly for the freezer.

*Choose only young plump pheasants for this dish. Older birds are not suitable as the meat
will dry up and become tough and chewy.*

Cut the pheasants in half. I like to remove the backbones at this stage, and discard them. Pull the legs and wings outwards until the half birds lie almost flat.

Chop the garlic into small pieces. Chop the bacon into small pieces. Grate the butter and combine it with the garlic, bacon, flour, salt and pepper.

Place the stretched pheasants on a baking tray, and cover evenly with the flour mixture.

Peel the potatoes and cut into even wedges. Place in a suitable ovenproof dish, and pour the chicken stock over them. Place the pheasant baking tray and the potato dish together in the oven preheated to 180°C/350°F/Gas 4, and cook for 40 minutes.

Remove the pheasants from the oven. They should be golden brown and slightly crunchy on top. Arrange on a serving plate and keep hot. Place the baking tray on a low flame and add the cream. Mix with the juices and flour residues using a spatula, and season with salt and pepper.

Meanwhile your potatoes should be ready; the chicken stock will have been absorbed, and the potato wedges should be slightly brown on the outside. Arrange beside the pheasants, and spoon the sauce on to the plate.

Serves 4

2 young plump
   pheasants
8 garlic cloves, peeled
4 back rashers bacon
2 oz (55 g) Irish butter,
   cold
4 oz (110 g) plain flour
salt and pepper
7 fl oz (200 ml) single
   cream

POTATOES
2 lb (900 g) old
   potatoes
¼ pint (150 ml) chicken
   stock

from the
HEDGEROWS

Hedgerows, some of them very old, are a particularly charming feature of the Irish countryside. They haven't been grubbed out to make large fields as elsewhere, so old varieties of hedge still flourish, and birds and small creatures have a safe habitat.

When walking the byways of *Ballykissangel*, you will see a large variety of wild fruit, nuts and berries in the hedgerows, especially in the autumn. There are bitter crab apples (for jelly or wine), even more bitter sloes (to flavour Christmas gin), damsons (for jam, or indeed a crumble if sweetened enough), rowanberries and elderberries and, occasionally, the medlar, a type of wild apple (jellies again). There are also chestnuts and hazelnuts and a favourite of mine, the giant puffball. These fungi grow under nettles and along the hedgerows, and can be tiny or huge, usually the latter.

Once upon a time these foods of the wild would have been an accepted part of the diet, but old traditions died, and it is only nowadays that people seem to be getting interested again. Over the years Irish country doctors, men like Michael Ryan in *Ballykissangel,* have maintained a policy of informing their patients about the benefits of seeking out natural foods and making them part of the daily diet. Nowadays, however, all the ingredients are freely available in shops and supermarkets, some virtually all year round.

As a child I was taught to collect these gifts of nature for my mother, who seemed to be endlessly boiling, bottling and baking. Sometimes I would get a clip on the ear instead of a friendly welcome, depending on how much I had dilly-dallied on the way home. I still remember her hazelnut biscuits though, and today my children love them too.

Soda Bread with Hazelnuts

*I*rish soda bread is famous worldwide, but it was only in the nineteenth century that the bread soda or bicarbonate of soda essential for its success was introduced. Before that, raising agents for breads included fermented potato juice.

This is one of my favourite breads, and it accompanies mushrooms in the photograph on pages 46–7. It is wonderful fresh from the oven and toasted the following day (if there is any left). You could add cashews or other nuts instead of the hazelnuts, or raisins or sultanas, or indeed leave them out altogether.

Makes 2 small loaves

1½ lb (675 g) plain flour
1 tsp salt
1 tsp bicarbonate of
  soda (bread soda)
3 oz (80 g) shelled
  hazelnuts, roughly
  chopped (or any raw
  nut of your choice)
½–¾ pint (300–450 ml)
  buttermilk

Mix the flour, salt, bicarbonate of soda and nuts together in a bowl. Make a well in the centre, add just under half the buttermilk and mix. The mixture should be firm and dryish. Add more milk until the mixture almost spreads out on its own.

Divide the mixture into two equal parts, and shape into rounds. Place on a baking tray, and cut a deep cross on the top of both. Place in a preheated oven at 200°C/400°F/Gas 6 for about 40 minutes. Test by tapping (you are wanting a hollow sound), or by using a skewer (which should come out dry).

When cooked, remove from the oven and allow to cool on a wire rack, which makes for a nice crusty loaf. If you want a soft crust, wrap the loaf in a clean teatowel before placing on the rack.

Pan-fried Puffballs

*T*his mushroom dish is one to invite your friends over for. The mushrooms that grow in the hedgerow are the giant puffball variety, and as they can reach 55 lb (25 kg) or so, you are not going to eat this monster on your own. Get on the phone!

Serves a lot

1 giant puffball, as fresh
   as possible
flour seasoned with salt
   and pepper
Irish butter

Peel off the outer skin of the mushrooms, and slice into steaks ½ in (1 cm) thick. Dredge the steaks with seasoned flour and simply fry on both sides in butter until golden brown.

Allow 3 steaks per person. Do the same the next day, the day after that, and . . .

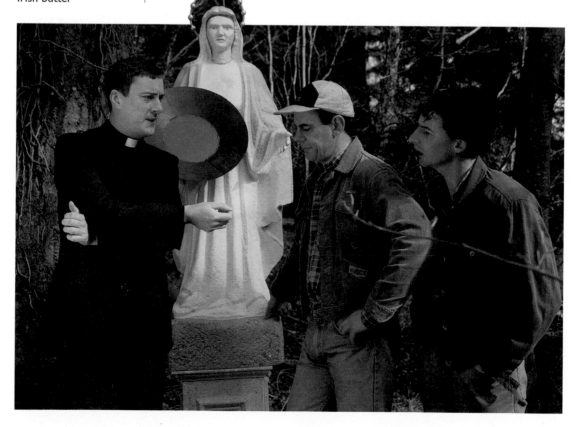

Blackberry (or Gooseberry) Crumble

*T*his is a hedgerow favourite. As a child, I used to love eating it straight from the oven, and then all the way through the day until it was gone!

Trim the blackberries (or top, tail and wash the gooseberries). Place in a 10 in (25 cm) pie dish and sprinkle with the sugar.

Put the crumble ingredients in a mixing bowl and rub together until the consistency of breadcrumbs. Spread the mixture evenly over the fruit and lightly press down with the back of your fingers. Place in the oven preheated to 180°C/350°F/Gas 4 and bake for 40 minutes until the crumble topping is golden brown.

Serve with whipped cream, ice cream or custard. Sprinkle with more caster sugar if a sweeter taste is required.

Serves 4

1½ lb (675 g) blackberries (or gooseberries)
2 oz (55 g) sugar

CRUMBLE TOPPING
3 oz (80 g) plain flour
1½ oz (40 g) Irish butter
1 oz (25 g) soft brown sugar
½ tsp ground cinnamon
1½ oz (40 g) shelled walnuts, chopped

Hazelnut Biscuits

*T*he hedgerows in Wicklow are studded with mature hazelnut trees, and the abundance of fruit sadly falls to the wayside or is eaten by the native red squirrel. I have made many recipes with hazelnuts, but biscuits like my mother used to make are my favourite. You can see them in the photograph on page 117.

Makes 30 biscuits

6 oz (175 g) hazelnuts
   in the shell
8 oz (225 g) fine
   wholemeal flour
8 oz (225 g) caster
   sugar
8 oz (225 g) Irish butter
1 egg white
4 oz (110 g) icing sugar,
   sieved

Shell the hazelnuts and roast them in the oven preheated to 200°C/400°F/Gas 6 for 3 minutes. Remove and allow to cool for a bit, then roughly chop. Leave to get cold.

Mix the flour, caster sugar, chopped hazelnuts and butter together, and knead very well until a dough is formed. Shape into a bar 2 in (5 cm) thick and 8 in (20 cm) long. Wrap in clingfilm and refrigerate for at least 1 hour, or freeze for 30 minutes.

Combine the egg white and icing sugar. Remove the dough from the fridge and slice into 30 rounds of about ¼ in (5 mm) thick. Arrange these rounds on a baking sheet.

Brush the biscuits with the egg white glaze and place in the preheated oven at 160°C/325°F/Gas 3 for 25–30 minutes.

Remove from the oven and allow to cool on a wire rack. Store in an airtight container, and eat at any time.

Hedgerow Pudding

If you have a sweet tooth, you will need extra sugar as hedgerow fruits have a tendency to be rather bitter. You can use sliced white or brown bread, but white is better as it shows up the colours. See the photograph on page 66.

Serves 4

Irish butter

6–8 slices bread, trimmed

3 oz (80 g) blackberries

3 oz (80 g) fraughans or blueberries

3 oz (80 g) redcurrants

3 oz (80 g) dark brown sugar

1 tbsp lemon juice

Grease the inside of a 1 lb (450 g) pudding bowl with softened butter. Press sliced bread against the sides to completely cover the inside of the pudding bowl. Leave a little bread for the top.

Mix the fruit, sugar and lemon juice and pour into the bread-lined pudding bowl. Cover with the remaining bread. Cover the top with foil and steam for 30 minutes in a steamer.

Remove from the steamer and allow to cool for a few minutes. Turn out by placing a plate on top of the bowl and inverting it. Serve with whipped cream as a wicked treat.

Apple and Blackberry Pie

*T*radition has it that it is unlucky to pick blackberries until September is out and then you mustn't pick them after Hallowe'en on 31 October, as the pooka (the devil elsewhere) will spit on them. Today, however, blackberries can be enjoyed all year round.

Make the pastry as described on page 18. Use half of it to line a pie plate and bake blind as on page 18.

To make the filling, slice the apples and place in a pot with the sugar and water. Heat gently until the apples have softened a bit, and the sugar has dissolved. Remove from the heat and add the blackberries. Stir through the apple, then pour over the cooked pastry. Cover with the remaining pastry, trim the edges, and press together. Paint with beaten egg, and bake in the preheated oven at 200°C/400°F/Gas 6 for 20 minutes or until golden brown. Remove from the oven, sprinkle with caster sugar, and serve with whipped cream or ice cream.

Serves 4

Shortcrust Pastry
    (see Fraughan Pie on
    page 18)

FILLING

3 large cooking apples
    (Bramleys are good),
    peeled
2 tbsp sugar
    (any kind will do)
2 tbsp water
1 lb (450 g) blackberries

TO FINISH
1 egg, beaten
caster sugar

from the
COASTLINES

The coastlines of Wicklow consist of many beautiful and peaceful sandy beaches and rolling sand dunes. In the early morning, before the families and their dogs arrive, and in the evening, when they have all gone home, the beaches from Bray to Arklow are great for shore angling. In the winter they can catch whiting and codling, in the summer bass and flat fish like dabs and plaice, with the occasional prize of an inshore conger eel. This type of fishing is a fairly recent phenomenon, but of course people have been taking boats out and scouring the seashores for food since the beginning of time.

Fish was eaten in Ireland primarily on fast days, and there are many traditional recipes. Most of these are for salted fish such as herring – once a great staple (but stocks are lower now) – and dried and salted cod or ling. Fresh fish was a luxury, but if salted it would last through the winter when other protein foods were scarce. Like corned beef and pork, salted cod and ling were exported to England, mainly from Cork, leaving smaller fish or the offal – such as cod's roe – for the local people. The 'walnuts' in the recipe on page 88 are a similar type of frugal food, and they are traditional in my family. There was a man in Dublin market who got the skins, heads and backbones of fish free; he would cut out the 'walnuts' from skate and ray heads (the muscles behind the eyes, or the cheeks), and sell them to discerning customers like my grandmother. The meat is soft and flavourful, but she used to say the monkfish ones were a bit tough.

Since freshness amounts to an obsession with those who cook seafood dishes in Ireland, Siobhan was well off the target, in an episode of *Ballykissangel,* when she assumed that a barmaid's appendicitis was really seafood poisoning! Shellfish such as oysters, mussels, scallops, cockles and crab flourish all round the Irish coast. Irish oysters are natives, in season when there is an 'R' in the month; Irish scallops are less common now because of dredging, but they can still occasionally be found. Once naturally plentiful, mussels are farmed all round the coast, but most cockles are still gathered in the time-honoured way, by digging them up out of the sand with a spoon. When I went to northern France, I saw several old people going on to the beach as the tide went out. They were all armed with spoons, and I knew exactly what they were doing!

Oysters and Mussels in Guinness

*T*his recipe is a real treat, but caution is needed with both the oysters and the mussels. *Thoroughly clean the shells, and place the mussels in cold water. The shells that float are discarded and any open ones are also discarded.*

Ten minutes may seem like a long time, but the Guinness bubbles up and doesn't reach the same temperature so quickly as water or wine would.

Serves 4

16 oysters, well
   scrubbed
24 mussels, well
   scrubbed
½ oz (15 g) Irish butter
2 garlic cloves, peeled
   and finely chopped
½ pint (300 ml) bottle
   or can of Guinness
chopped parsley

In a large pot with a lid, melt the butter and gently brown the garlic. Toss the oysters and mussels into the pot and stir. Pour the Guinness over the shells and cover the pot with the lid. Boil for 10 minutes.

Serve steaming in large soup bowls, garnished with the parsley. Garlic bread is good to mop up the juices, as we've done in the photograph on pages 76–7.

80   ◆

Cockles with Mushrooms

*C*ollecting cockles was a family tradition. My mother would arm each of us with an old spoon, show us how to dig them up, then she would talk to the neighbours while we and the neighbours' children spent hours digging and collecting. The cockles were brought home, then cleaned and boiled for 10 minutes. The cockle meat was scraped from the shell (often with the same spoon you dug them up with) and kept warm until all the cockles were done. They were seasoned with salt, white pepper and lemon juice, and then the mixture was spread on to buttered white sliced bread. The bread was folded over, and the sandwich was eaten backwards by holding the fold in the bread and biting through the crust. This ensured that the juices were in the sandwich, not on your clothes.

Mussels or scallops could be used instead of the cockles.

Thoroughly clean the cockles. Place in a pot, cover with cold water, then bring to the boil, reduce the heat and simmer until the shells open, about 10 minutes. Plunge into cold water, then drain very well. Remove the cockle meat from the shells, and discard the shells.

Slice the onion and garlic and gently fry in the butter for a few minutes. Add the bacon and fry until brown, then add the mushrooms and the lemon juice. Cook for 2 minutes, then add the cream and the cockle meat. Bring to the boil, reduce the heat and simmer for 2 minutes. Season with salt and pepper.

Serve on a bed of rice and garnish each plate with a whole cooked Dublin Bay prawn if you like.

Serves 4

6 lb (2.75 kg) fresh cockles, or 2 lb (900 g) cockle meat

1 medium onion, peeled

1 garlic clove, peeled

1 oz (25 g) Irish butter

4 mild smoked rashers bacon, chopped (hickory flavour is good)

8 oz (225 g) small button mushrooms, wiped

juice of 1 lemon

¼ pint (150 ml) single cream

salt and pepper

Whiting and Scallops with Lemon and Dill Sauce

Whiting is one of the commoner sea fish on Ireland's east coast. If you go fishing, it's a fair probability that the first ten fish you land will be whiting.

Traditionally this dish was a fish stew, with potatoes, carrots, turnip and barley in it. Rather bland, but very filling for growing lads.

Serves 4

8 medium whiting fillets

24 medium shelled scallops (fresh or frozen)

½ pint (300 ml) chicken stock

2 whole lemons, cut in quarters

2 oz (55 g) Irish butter

¼ pint (150 ml) single cream

4 sprigs fresh dill or 1 tsp dried dill

salt and pepper

4 spring onions, finely chopped

Bring the chicken stock up to the boil in a large pot, then place in the whiting fillets, skin side up. Bring back to the boil, and add the scallops and lemon quarters. Bring back to the boil again, then add the butter and cream. Bring back to the boil, then reduce the heat.

Season with the dill, salt and pepper, then simmer to reduce the liquid by half. The whole cooking process takes about 10 minutes altogether.

Arrange the fish and scallops and their juices on serving plates and garnish with the chopped spring onion. Serve with garlic bread. Delicious!

Cod Steak with Tarragon, Prawns and Garlic Sauce

*C*od and codling come into the Irish Sea to feed. The fish are very large in the winter, very much smaller (about 2–3 lb/1–1.4 kg) in the summer.

For this recipe you will need thin steaks cut from the top of a big fish. Make sure that all the bones are removed, as cod bones when cooked are like sewing needles.

Mix the breadcrumbs, tarragon, prawns, lemon juice and onion. Season with salt and pepper. Divide in four, and place into the 'hole' in the cod steaks, 4 prawns per steak. Melt the butter in a pan, sprinkle the cod steaks with flour, and gently fry the steaks until golden brown on both sides, about 10 minutes. Remove from the pan and keep hot.

Chop the garlic and fry in the same pan, then add the cream and season with salt and pepper. Bring to the boil, reduce the heat and simmer for 1 minute, stirring all the time.

Arrange the cod steaks on serving plates, and spoon over the sauce. Garnish with some extra tarragon leaves.

Serves 4

4 × 6 oz (175 g) cod
   steaks, 1 in (2.5 cm)
   thick
4 oz (110 g)
   breadcrumbs
4 sprigs fresh tarragon,
   chopped, or 2 tsp
   dried tarragon
16 shelled prawns
   (fresh or frozen)
2 tbsp lemon juice
2 small onions, peeled
   and finely chopped
salt and pepper
2 oz (55 g) Irish butter
a little plain flour
2 garlic cloves, peeled
¼ pint (150 ml) single
   cream

Pan-fried Dabs with Spinach and Onion

Dabs are flat fish like plaice or sole, and on our Wicklow coastline are plentiful and easily caught. Although small in size, they are extremely tasty. You can cook dabs whole on the bone, but I like to use only the fillets.

You can substitute plaice or sole in this recipe.

Serves 4

1¼–1½ lb (550–675 g) dab fillets (from small fish, about 4 fillets per person)

2 oz (55 g) plain flour

1 egg, beaten

2 garlic cloves, peeled and finely chopped

¼ pint (150 ml) milk

1 oz (25 g) Irish butter

1 large onion, peeled and roughly chopped

2 oz (55 g) spinach leaves, washed

salt and pepper

corn oil

TO SERVE

2 tbsp chopped parsley

4 lemon wedges

Mix the flour, egg, chopped garlic and milk to make a light batter. Allow to stand in the fridge for at least 30 minutes.

Melt the butter in a pan and cook the onion until tender and transparent. Add the spinach and cover the pan until the spinach has wilted and cooked, about 5 minutes. Season with salt and pepper and mix well with a sharp knife, slicing the spinach mixture roughly. Keep hot.

Dip the dab fillets in the batter and shallow-fry in hot oil until golden brown.

Strain the spinach and make a mound in the centre of each serving plate. Place the cooked dab fillets neatly around the mound, and garnish with parsley and lemon wedges.

Poached Conger Eel with Onions and Garlic

This voracious fish is disliked by fishermen because they take the lobsters from pots, but they are much sought after by sea anglers. The eels also get caught in fishing nets and end up on market stalls, where they used to be sold off very cheaply. They were not regarded as suitable for the table because of their tough skin and unusual bone structure.

The traditional way of cooking conger was to stew it with carrots, onions and potatoes, a hearty meal for the hungry, which tasted like fishy potatoes. Try this recipe instead. Any other white or flaky poached fish could be served with this sauce.

Remove the head and tail from the eel. Cut the eel lengthways through the backbone. Rinse under cold water to remove any pieces of bone, and any blood. Place in a roasting tin skin side down. Pour the boiling water over the backbone of the eel. Cover with foil and place in a preheated oven at 200°C/400°F/Gas 6 for 10 minutes. Take out of the oven and remove the foil. Carefully drain the liquid from the roasting tin and remove the backbone from each side of the eel. This is done by holding down the meat with one hand and easing the backbone up with the other. Cut each side across in half and remove the skin. Carefully invert on to a serving plate and keep warm.

Melt the butter in a pan and lightly brown the whole onions. Chop the garlic and add to the pan, along with the cream and tarragon, salt and pepper. Bring to the boil, reduce the heat and simmer for 2 minutes.

Spoon the sauce over the fish, and serve garnished with some extra chopped tarragon and a crisp salad, or boiled potatoes and carrots for the really hungry!

Serves 4

1 conger eel, weighing
　5–6 lb (2.25–2.75 kg)
2 pints (1.2 litres)
　boiling water
2 oz (55 g) Irish butter
16 silverskin (pickling)
　onions, peeled
2 garlic cloves, peeled
¼ pint (150 ml) single
　cream
2 sprigs fresh tarragon
salt and pepper

Crab Cakes with Parsley Sauce

*C*rabs used to be thought of as a pest, as they would get into the lobster pots, but they are much more popular now. Straight from the sea, I can't think of anything tastier.

This is a variation on the traditional fish cake. I make them with the sweet meat from the claws, but you could use the whole crab or canned or frozen white crab meat. If using fresh claws, plunge them into a large pot half filled with boiling water and hard-boil for 4 minutes. Drain and allow to cool, then crack claws with a nutcracker, and remove meat with a boning knife or tweezers.

The small cakes make a perfect starter. Form larger cakes for a main course.

Serves 4

6 large crab claws or
    8 oz (225 g) canned
    or frozen crab meat
4 medium potatoes
salt and pepper
1 egg, beaten with a
    little milk
1 oz (25 g) medium
    oatflakes
corn oil

SAUCE
½ oz (15 g) Irish butter
1 tsp cornflour
¼ pint (150 ml) milk
¼ pint (150 ml) chicken
    stock
6 sprigs parsley, finely
    chopped

Cook the crab claws, and then remove the meat. Boil the potatoes, then mash and leave to cool.

Mix the crab meat with the mashed potato, then season with salt and pepper. Form into small cakes 2 in (5 cm) in diameter and 1 in (2.5 cm) thick. Dip the cakes in the beaten egg then roll in the oatflakes. Fry in shallow hot oil until golden brown (be careful not to burn them). Keep hot.

For the parsley sauce, melt the butter in a pot, and add the cornflour. Stir in, then add the milk and chicken stock. Bring to the boil and simmer, stirring, until smooth and creamy. Add the parsley and allow to infuse.

Pour the parsley sauce on to serving plates and place the crab cakes on top. Serve immediately.

'Walnuts' and Fried Bread

M y grandmother on my father's side loved to cook fish, and when we went over for tea, she always gave us this tasty dish. As a child I liked the taste of these boneless and skinless chunks of fish and accepted the explanation that 'They are the best bit of the ray, and they are only for children'. It wasn't until I re-created the dish as an adult that I discovered the true origins of the meat (see page 78). Just as well – what child would knowingly eat them?

Chunks of a firm fish like monkfish would be good cooked in the same way.

Serves 4

4 thin slices white bread

Irish butter

4 streaky rashers bacon

1 lemon

8–10 'walnuts'
   (or pieces of firm fish),
   about 8 oz (225 g) in
   weight per person

¼ pint (150 ml) single
   cream

salt and pepper

Lightly butter the sliced bread on both sides. Fry the slices until golden brown on both sides, then keep warm in the low oven at about 150°C/300°F/Gas 2. Fry the bacon in the bread pan until cooked and nearly crisp. Place the rashers on top of the bread slices, and return to the oven to allow the rashers to crisp up.

Cut the peel off half the lemon, and slice it finely. Squeeze the juice.

Reheat the pan with the butter and bacon fat, and place the 'walnuts' in it. Fry on both sides for about 1 minute. Add the lemon peel and the lemon juice, then the cream and about ½ oz (15 g) butter. Stir until smooth and creamy.

Take the rashers off the bread, and chop them up. Pour the 'walnuts' and sauce on top of each piece of fried bread, and sprinkle the chopped bacon on top as a garnish. Serve to your children, but don't tell them what the 'walnuts' are!

Cod's Roe with Bacon

*F*resh cod's roe can be found occasionally in fishmongers' shops between January and April; it is also available smoked. It is a favourite breakfast dish in Ireland, cooked as below, with bacon and perhaps some fried potatoes, but it can also be deep-fried in a light batter, or made into a type of soufflé.

Wrap the cod's roe loosely in a piece of muslin and gently simmer for 30 minutes in fish stock to cover. Remove from the liquid and allow to cool. When cold, slice into 8 × ½ in (1 cm) steaks.

Season the flour with salt, pepper and lemon rind. Dip both sides of the cod's roe steaks in the seasoned flour and fry in the butter on both sides until golden. Remove from the pan. Wrap a bacon rasher, bottom to top, around each steak and place the steaks on a baking tray. Butterfly the tomatoes (cutting them in half, but not quite through), sprinkle with sea salt and a few drops of olive oil, and place beside the cod's roe steaks. Bake in the oven preheated to 200°C/400°F/Gas 6 for 15 minutes.

Arrange cod's roe steaks and tomatoes on a breakfast plate and garnish with a wedge of lemon, or serve with a crisp salad and brown soda bread for lunch.

Serves 4

1½ lb (675 g) cod's roe

fish stock to cover

2 tbsp plain flour

salt and pepper

finely grated rind of
   1 lemon

1 oz (25 g) Irish butter

8 back rashers bacon

8 tomatoes

sea salt

olive oil

from the
FARMS

In the many farms in Wicklow and around *Ballykissangel*, the farmer is a great man. His wife is not to be spoken to about business, but in most cases, of course, she will be running the show! Traditionally she would be the daughter of another farmer, and would have supplied her husband with a dowry of a few extra acres of land. Her knowledge would have been handed down from her mother and her mother before her, thus the recipes would be so unchanged that her breads, stews and vegetable soups are almost tradition itself.

One of her most important tasks was to look after the chickens, and every farm and many individual households would have a henhouse. My grandmother had eighteen hens and one cock, and it used to be my job to collect the eggs. As the birds were allowed to roam free around the farmyard (and often inside the house as well), you never quite knew where the eggs might be. These free-range eggs were used in many ways – fried with bacon was particularly popular, and not just for breakfast.

Every farm and many villagers would also have a pigsty, and its occupants would eat all the leftovers and rubbish. A pig would be killed in the autumn (unless it belonged to *Ballykissangel*'s Eamonn Byrne, a man to whom pigs are beloved members of the family), and not a piece of it would be wasted; the head would be salted or made into brawn; the trotters would be made into the dish called crubeens (a speciality of Cork, after the prime meats were sent abroad), or steamed (see page 108); the meat would be eaten fresh, or salted for bacon; the offal would be variously fried or stewed; and the blood would be used in sausage and pudding making. In fact, bacon and cabbage is much more common in Ireland, much more representative of how the Irish really eat, than the more famous Irish stew.

The Irish Omelette

*M*y grandfather's claim to the kitchen was this humble dish which he called 'egg cake'. It consisted of only four ingredients – sliced potatoes, onion, eggs and streaky bacon. He would fry the bacon on both sides until it was burnt, and mix it with the other ingredients. At this stage he would remove the frying pan from the heat and replace it with a cast-iron lid which he left until it got very hot. When the bacon had stopped sizzling, he would pour the egg mixture into the pan and cover the pan with the hot lid. This went back on to a low heat for 20 minutes. It had a tendency to be very brown on the outside and the potatoes were sometimes a bit raw, but the taste was delicious!

Instead of slicing the potatoes, grate them, and remove the excess moisture by squeezing them in a clean teatowel. Beat the eggs well, then mix with the grated potato. Place the onion, garlic and butter in a skillet (or an ovenproof frying pan), and gently fry until they are transparent. Remove from the skillet and mix with the potato and egg. Season with salt and pepper.

Arrange the bacon rashers on the bottom of the skillet and pour the egg mixture on top. Place the skillet into a preheated oven at 200°C/400°F/Gas 6 and bake for 10–15 minutes. When set, turn out by placing a plate on the top of the pan and turning the pan upside down. Serve in slices with lettuce and sliced tomatoes.

Serves 4

2 lb (900 g) potatoes,
   peeled
6 eggs, beaten
1 large onion, peeled
   and coarsely chopped
1 garlic clove, peeled
   and chopped
½ oz (15 g) Irish butter
salt and pepper
10 streaky rashers
   bacon

Vegetable Soup

Traditionally this dish was a 'filler' during the working day. It's really a stew, with whole potatoes and onions added for an hour along with whatever vegetables you had to hand – carrots, turnips, peas, cabbage, celery, and, occasionally, barley for those extra cold days. It was served with lots of bread and butter, and it was very tasty and filling. As my grandfather used to say, 'Sure, there's eating and drinking in this soup!'

Serves 4

4 large potatoes

2 carrots

2 large cabbage leaves

2 celery sticks

2 medium onions

½ medium turnip

8 oz (225 g) garden
   peas

4 oz (110 g) pearl
   barley

2½ pints (1.4 litres)
   water

salt and pepper

2 sprigs parsley

1 sprig thyme

6 sage leaves

Peel and wash the vegetables as appropriate. Place the barley in a pot, and cover with the cold water. Bring to the boil, reduce the heat and simmer for 10 minutes.

Chop the vegetables into large pieces (the potatoes and onions in half), and place in the pot. Add salt and pepper and the herbs, bring back to the boil, reduce the heat and simmer until the potatoes are cooked, about 20–30 minutes.

Spoon into wide-rimmed soup bowls, and serve with home-made soda or buttermilk bread (see pages 69 or 101) or garlic bread.

FROM THE FARMS

Baked Eggs

This simple dish is very tasty indeed, and is perfect for vegetarians. My mother used to cook it whenever a particular friend of my sister came round. The possible variations on the theme are endless.

Chop the celery, potato and carrot finely. Place in a pot, cover with water, and bring to the boil. Simmer for 5 minutes, then drain and place in a large ovenproof soup bowl. Slice the mushrooms, garlic and spring onion and gently fry in the butter. Remove from the heat and put into the soup bowl. Slice the tomato and place on top of the other vegetables.

Put the cornflour in a pan and stir in the juices from the vegetables. Add the milk and bring to the boil, stirring all the time. Season with salt and pepper and pour over the vegetables.

Place the soup bowl in the preheated oven at 160°C/325°F/Gas 3 for 15 minutes. The mixture should be starting to bubble. Remove from the oven, and with the back of a spoon make two dents by pressing firmly down. Crack the eggs into the dents. Sprinkle with a little grated cheese and return to the oven for 4–5 minutes. The cheese should be melted and the eggs set but not hard.

Garnish with celery leaves and serve with brown bread. Caution is recommended as this dish is extremely hot.

Per person

1 celery stick (keep the
   leaves)
1 medium potato,
   peeled
1 very small carrot or
   ¼ medium carrot
2 small mushrooms
1 garlic clove, peeled
1 spring onion
½ oz (15 g) Irish butter
1 small tomato
1 tsp cornflour
¼ pint (150 ml) milk
salt and pepper
2 eggs
a little grated cheese

Bacon and Cabbage in Cider

There was a time, not too long ago, when bacon with cabbage was the staple diet of many an Irish family. This diet was only broken on Fridays, as Friday was a day of fast, when meat was not allowed to be consumed.

Bacon with cabbage is still eaten today, and with a greater variety of cabbages and better curing methods, gives you a more versatile recipe.

Serves 4

2 lb (900 g) lean back
   bacon in the piece
1 small head white
   cabbage, about 2 lb
   (900 g)
1½ pints (900 ml) dry
   cider
4 bay leaves
12 black peppercorns

Steep the bacon in cold water to cover for 2–3 hours, then drain and rinse well. Cover the bacon with fresh cold water, bring to the boil, and simmer for 15 minutes. Remove the bacon from the water (which you keep), and place the bacon in a casserole. Cover with cider, and add the bay leaves and peppercorns. Put the lid on the casserole and place in the preheated oven at 140°C/275°F/Gas 1 for 2 hours.

Meanwhile, slice the cabbage into ¼ in (5 mm) strips and put into the bacon water. Bring to the boil and simmer for 15 minutes or until the cabbage is tender.

Remove the casserole from the oven. You will find the cider almost gone. Remove the meat from the dish, and slice into 4 thick steaks. Drain the cabbage and arrange on serving plates. Place the bacon on top of the cabbage. Serve immediately with potatoes or Colcannon (see page 24) as in the photograph on pages 90–91.

Savoury Snow Eggs

*T*his dish is a variation on the baked eggs on page 95, but is really only a snack, although it's tasty at any time of the day.

Serves 4

4 oz (110 g) white
  Cheddar cheese

1 tbsp fine mustard

2 oz (55 g) cooked ham

4 eggs

salt and pepper

lots of chopped parsley

Chop the cheese and place in an ovenproof dish. Spread mustard over the cheese. Chop the ham and place on top of the mustard and cheese. Place the dish in a preheated oven at 180°C/350°F/Gas 4 for about 8 minutes.

Separate the eggs, then beat the yolks and season with salt, pepper and parsley. Pour over the cheese and ham mixture. Return to the oven for about 5 minutes. Whisk the egg whites until very stiff then spoon on top of the mixture. Reduce the oven heat to 140°C/275°F/Gas 1 and bake for 10 minutes.

Garnish with more parsley, and serve with garlic bread.

Rasher Chops with Onion and Mushroom Sauce

*T*he local butcher's shop was the pick-up and drop-off point in the village – for things like away football matches, bingo, dances, trips to Dublin etc. In the window he had a bacon slicer and many a bus fare was won and lost by betting on the amount of rashers he would get from the piece of bacon on the slicer. The slicer was a great focal point, but alas, one day it broke!

For this recipe, ask your butcher to cut you 4 back rashers ¾ in (2 cm) thick. Cut off the rind and half the fat, and try not to guess how many rashers he would get!

Thoroughly rinse the chops in cold water then pat dry with kitchen paper. Place the chops in a pot, cover with milk, and season with mustard, thyme and black pepper. Bring to the boil, reduce the heat and simmer for about 15–20 minutes until nearly all the liquid is gone.

Remove the chops from the pot, and brush with egg wash. Coat with the breadcrumb and flour mixture, then place on a baking tray. Bake in the preheated oven at 180°C/350°F/Gas 4 for 15 minutes until golden brown and crunchy.

For the sauce, melt the butter in a large pan and cook the whole onions, stirring to avoid burning. When the onions are starting to soften, add the whole mushrooms and cook until they start to change colour. Add the cream, Irish Mist and salt, bring to the boil and remove from the heat.

Place 5 onions and 5 mushrooms on each plate, and spoon the remaining sauce over them. Place a rasher chop beside them. Serve with soda bread to mop up the delicious sauce.

Serves 4

4 back bacon chops

1 pint (600 ml) milk

1 tsp dry mustard

a pinch of dried thyme

black pepper

1 egg, mixed with a
   little milk

2 oz (55 g) breadcrumbs

1 tbsp plain flour

SAUCE

1 oz (25 g) Irish butter

20 very small silverskin
   (pickling) onions or
   shallots, peeled

20 medium button
   mushrooms

¼ pint (150 ml) single
   cream

2 tbsp Irish Mist liqueur

a pinch of salt

Pork Kidneys and Potatoes

This dish was originally made from potatoes boiled in their skins and allowed to go cold. The pork kidneys were sliced and fried in butter with the potatoes, turning them regularly to ensure the thorough cooking of the kidneys and the reheating of the potatoes. At this stage cream would be added and salt and pepper, then it would be brought to the boil and served in a bowl with a thick piece of bread to mop up the sauce from the base of the bowl. It was tasty, filling and very quick to make.

Serves 4

2 lb (900 g) new
  potatoes, scrubbed
salt and pepper
about 2 lb (900 g) pork
  kidneys, trimmed
¼ pint (150 ml) double
  cream
2 spring onions,
  chopped
chopped parsley

Boil the potatoes in salted water for 10 minutes, then drain and place in a roasting tin. Slice the kidneys and place on top of the potatoes. Bake for 10 minutes in an oven preheated to 200°C/400°F/Gas 6. Remove from the oven and pour over the cream. Season with salt and pepper, turn the mixture over, and return to the oven for a further 5 minutes.

Serve in a bowl garnished with the chopped spring onion and parsley.

Traditional Buttermilk Brown Bread

A s tradition has it, this buttermilk brown bread, which is made on farms and in villages all over Ireland, is as versatile as the Irish weather. This recipe is one I use all the time.

Makes 1 round loaf

1 lb (450 g) wholemeal
　flour
1 tbsp bran
1 tbsp cracked wheat
1 tsp bicarbonate of
　soda (bread soda)
½ tsp salt
½ pint (300 ml)
　buttermilk

Mix the dry ingredients in a mixing bowl, and add enough buttermilk to make a moist but firm dough.

Put on a baking tray and shape into a round. Cut a deep cross in the top of the dough, and then bake for 30 minutes in an oven preheated to 200°C/400°F/Gas 6. Reduce the oven temperature to 180°C/350°F/Gas 4 and continue baking for a further 20 minutes.

Test by tapping (the bread should sound hollow) or with a skewer (it should come out dry). You can vary the crust as with the soda bread on page 69. For best results, do not slice until thoroughly set, some 4 or 5 hours.

from the
VILLAGES

There are countless villages dotted throughout rural Wicklow, some better known than others. Avoca, which is the real *Ballykissangel*, has become famous, and is now thriving because of the series. It is representative of Irish village life to a great extent, which is presumably why the producers chose it. Its infrastructure is similar to that of other villages, having a church, shop and pub – the centre of all communities – as well as a garda station and post office to service the rest of the community. Sometimes, of course, in small villages the pub and shop would be confined to one building, and in my local bar, on the road between Avoca and The Old Coach House, they serve pints of Guinness at one end of the building one minute, and packets of cornflakes and soap at the other end a few minutes later.

Fitzgeralds – formerly The Fountain Bar – lies at the heart of Ballykissangel social life, as the pub does all over Ireland. It is here that many of Brian Quigley's schemes are hatched, where Brendan, Siobhan,

Niamh and their friends hear all the gossip, and where Assumpta and Father Clifford cross swords. If Assumpta still ran the pub in the old-fashioned way, she might have offered some traditional foods such as trotters or pork scratchings, guaranteed to increase sales of the black stuff! But time marches on. Nowadays Assumpta serves up a range of quick foods that includes Father Peter's favourite – tuna mix in a granary bap, easy on the mayonnaise.

The village too is where many traditional Irish recipes are remembered and re-created. Black puddings vary from place to place, and each is said to have its own secret ingredient (usually salt). Local butchers used to make them, as well as cook tripe, trotters and other meats, but this has ceased now. Village bakers still, however, sell local breads and cakes, often made from recipes which have been handed down for generations.

Pork Scratchings

Traditionally pubs in Ireland were segregated, and women were not allowed in many bars. In the men-only bars you were served up boiled pigs' tails and crubeens, boiled salted pig's trotters. The idea was that after eating these salty treats one would buy lots of pints. Today, however, the women are in, and the trotters are out (some say because the porter glasses would get too greasy!). Pork scratchings are served instead, and they are much easier to eat than trotters, but have the same result – lots of drink to quench the thirst!

You will need the back skin of the pig with all the fat removed. Slice the skin in 2 in (5 cm) strips ½ in (1 cm) wide. Place on a baking tray and sprinkle with salt and white pepper. Cook slowly in the oven preheated to 150°C/300°F/Gas 2 for 1 hour or until dry and crunchy. Allow to cool and then store in airtight containers.

FROM THE VILLAGES

Smoked Cod and Onions

*T*his traditional dish was a Friday night special, often actually eaten on the Saturday, as a stomach settler after the intake of the night before. . . It was quick and easy to make, filling and full of taste.

Slice the smoked cod into 1 in (2.5 cm) strips. Fry the onion in the butter until transparent. Add the smoked cod and the garlic and bay leaves. Blend a little milk with the cornflour, and add the remaining milk to the pan. Gently bring to the boil. Remove from the heat and stir in the cornflour mixture. Return to the heat and simmer for 5–10 minutes. Season to taste with salt and pepper.

Serve with boiled potatoes and garden peas.

Serves 4

2 lb (900 g) smoked
   cod
2 large onions, peeled
   and roughly chopped
1 oz (25 g) Irish butter
1 garlic clove, peeled
   and chopped
2 bay leaves
1 pint (600 ml) milk
1 tsp cornflour
salt and pepper

Steamed Trotters

*T*he humble and salty taste of the trotter has come a long way in this updated version of the traditional pub dish. The trotter has to be boned first, rather like removing the skin from a chicken's leg. You need to insert a small sharp knife between skin and bone, starting at the knee joint, then carefully cut around the bone and roll back the skin. Repeat this until you reach the toe joint. Simply cut through the ligaments and discard the bone. You will be left with a perfect casing.

Serves 4

4 pig's trotters,
   prepared (see above)

FILLING
1 medium onion, peeled
   and finely chopped
½ oz (15 g) Irish butter
1½ lb (675 g) minced
   pork
2 garlic cloves, peeled
   and finely chopped
8 medium button
   mushrooms, grated
8 sage leaves, finely
   chopped
salt and pepper
1 egg, beaten

TO FINISH
2 tomatoes, sliced
2 hard-boiled eggs, sliced

Fry the onion in the butter until soft. Allow to cool, and place in a mixing bowl. Add the minced pork, chopped garlic and grated mushrooms. Season with sage, salt and pepper. Add the egg to the mixture, mix thoroughly together, and fill the trotters almost to the top.

Tie the opening with string, at intervals along the length of the trotter, and place the trotters in a steamer. Steam for 20 minutes until the skin is tender. Remove from the steamer and slice the trotters into ½ in (1 cm) rounds. Discard the string pieces and toe.

Arrange the slices on a serving plate with sliced tomatoes and sliced hard-boiled egg.

Honeycomb Tripe with Cow's Heel

This traditional dish, usually served for Saturday tea, is delicious. When buying, make sure you only get the honeycomb tripe, from the second stomach of the cow, as it is much more tender than the tripe from the first stomach. Ask the butcher to order the cow heel for you, and to scald, clean and split it for you. The gelatine in the heel gives the stew a lovely richness.

For convenience, use two pots for boiling. Place the tripe and cow's heel in one pot, and cover with cold water. Add 1 tsp of salt and bring to the boil. Boil for 5 minutes, then drain, remove from the pot, and place in the other pot. Cover with water again, season with salt, and bring to the boil for 5 minutes. This procedure must be done three times in all, helping to cook the tripe and soften the heel. (Wash the empty pot in between boilings.)

After boiling the tripe three times, cut it into 2 in (5 cm) strips, and place back into the pot with the cow's heel. Add enough milk to cover, bring to the boil and simmer for about 30–40 minutes.

Mix the remaining milk with the cornflour and add to the simmering milk. Remove the cow's heel and discard. Bring the sauce back to the boil, reduce the heat and simmer for 5 minutes. Add the butter and salt and pepper to taste.

This dish is usually served with boiled potatoes, and although bland in appearance, it's certainly not in taste!

Serves 4

2 lb (900 g) honeycomb
  tripe
1 cow's heel
salt and pepper
2 pints (1.2 litres) milk
1 tsp cornflour
½ oz (15 g) Irish butter

Steak Sandwich

The steak sandwich would once be what awaited the pub drinker when he returned home late, the worse for wear – a shrivelled-up, cold piece of cooked meat which was fit for nothing but putting between two pieces of buttered bread. This modern version, a stalwart in many pubs today (see the photograph on page 102), would be well worth coming home on time for!

Per person

1 crunchy bread roll

1 tsp smooth mustard

1 tsp tomato ketchup

a few iceberg lettuce
leaves, shredded

1 medium tomato,
sliced

1 × 6 oz (175 g) fillet
steak

2 mushrooms, thinly
sliced

Irish butter

2–3 onion rings

a little mayonnaise

Cut the bread roll lengthways, and spread with mustard and ketchup. Cover with shredded lettuce and sliced tomato.

Cut the fillet steak into three thin steaks about ¼ in (5 mm) thick. Fry these steaks to your liking with the mushroom in a little butter. Place the cooked steaks on top of the tomatoes, and then the cooked mushrooms on top. Cover with onion rings and dot with mayonnaise. Top with the top of the roll.

Would you come home late for dinner?

Black Pudding

Ireland is famous for its black and white puddings and its sausages, and each village would have its own recipes. They were always made in bulk, thus the amounts given here, just in case you want to try making it yourself at home!

Strain the blood through muslin to remove threads. Needless to say, this blood should be as fresh as possible. Cube the flare fat and place in a wire sieve. Scald in boiling water. This is most important to prevent it spoiling. Mix the remaining ingredients in a large mixing bowl with the scalded fat and, finally, the blood. Mix very well and place in the casing. Twist off every 10 in (25 cm) or so. This is best done in a sausage machine, of course, but a piping bag or large funnel will do.

Place in a bain-marie and cook for 40 minutes in the oven preheated to 180°C/350°F/Gas 4. When cooked, hang up to dry, then refrigerate for up to 5 days. To reheat, cut into slices and fry as an integral part of an Irish Sunday breakfast (see page 120).

Makes about 10 lb (4.5 kg) puddings

3 pints (1.8 litres) pigs' blood

2 lb (900 g) flare fat (inside fat of pig stomach)

6 oz (175 g) cooked pearl barley

7 oz (200 g) plain flour

7 oz (200 g) fine oatmeal

4 oz (110 g) onions, peeled and chopped

7 oz (200 g) salt

2 oz (55 g) ground black pepper

¼ oz (8 g) celery seeds

1 oz (25 g) paprika

1 oz (25 g) ground coriander

1 oz (25 g) dry mustard powder

pudding casing (get from your butcher)

Brown Yeast Bread

*T*his bread is dense and nutritious, and with the seeds in, it almost has the consistency of cake. It is best made with fresh yeast but dried yeast is more easily available and easier to use.

I like this bread while it is still hot, when the butter melts very easily on it, and toasted for breakfast.

Makes 1 × 2 lb (900 g) loaf

2 tsp dried yeast

2 tsp light brown sugar

12 fl oz (350 ml) lukewarm water

1 lb 2 oz (500 g) fine wholemeal flour

1 tsp salt

1 tsp sunflower seeds

1 tsp pumpkin seeds

1 tsp sesame seeds

Reconstitute the yeast by putting it and the sugar into the lukewarm water and leaving in a warm place for 10–15 minutes. (You could of course also use the easy dried yeast that you put in with the flour.)

In a mixing bowl mix the flour, salt, sunflower and pumpkin seeds. Pour in the reconstituted yeast, and mix well. The mixture should be quite wet, so scoop into a greased 2 lb (900 g) loaf tin and pat level with the back of a wet finger.

Sprinkle the top of the bread with the sesame seeds and leave in a warm place to double in size, about 20–25 minutes. (You can place the tin of dough in an oiled plastic bag to assist in this rising.)

When risen, put the loaf in a preheated hot oven at 200°C/400°F/Gas 6 for 30 minutes. Test by tapping (you want a hollow sound) or with a skewer (if this comes out dry, the bread is ready). Allow to cool on a wire rack.

Irish Porter Cake

*T*his is rather like a heavy tea brack, rich and moist, but it would make an excellent Christmas or christening cake when iced. Guinness is used as porter, a form of stout which is not made nowadays. Make sure the Guinness is at room temperature.

Makes 1 × 9 in (23 cm) cake

225 g (8 oz) Irish butter

1 lb (450 g) plain flour

1 lb (450 g) light brown sugar

1½ lb (675 g) mixed currants, raisins and sultanas

4 oz (110 g) glacé cherries

4 oz (110 g) chopped almonds

4 oz (110 g) mixed peel

finely grated rind of 1 lemon

a pinch of mixed spice

1 egg, beaten

½ pint (300 ml) Guinness, at room temperature

1 level tsp bicarbonate of soda

2 fl oz (55 ml) Irish whiskey

Rub the butter into the flour until it resembles fine breadcrumbs. Add all the other dry ingredients and mix well. Beat the egg and the Guinness together and add the bicarbonate of soda. Mix this very well into the dry cake mixture. Add the whiskey, and stir that well in too.

Turn the mixture into a greased and lined 9 in (23 cm) cake tin, cover with greaseproof paper and bake in a slow oven preheated to 150°C/300°F/Gas 2 for 2 hours. Reduce the temperature to 140°C/275°F/Gas 1 and bake for a further 1–1½ hours.

Test by piercing the centre with a skewer; if it comes out clean the cake is done. The cake will also have shrunk from the sides of the tin. Cool on a rack, then store in an airtight tin.

Irish Mist Mousse

A delicious after-dinner treat, featuring Irish Mist, a herb and honey liqueur based on Irish whiskey.

Serves 4

2 tsp water

2 tsp powdered gelatine

3 eggs, separated

3 oz (80 g) caster sugar

½ pint (300 ml) double cream

2 fl oz (55 ml) Irish Mist liqueur

Place the 2 tsp water in a small heatproof bowl and sprinkle the gelatine on to the liquid. Stand the bowl over a saucepan of hot water and stir the gelatine until it has dissolved completely. Cool slightly.

Beat the egg yolks and the sugar together until pale and creamy. In another bowl beat the egg whites until stiff. Lightly beat the cream in yet another small bowl. Add the gelatine and Irish Mist to the egg and sugar mixture, and thoroughly mix together. Add the whipped cream and lastly fold in the egg whites with a metal spoon. Spoon into individual ramekins or dariole moulds, or into a large dessert bowl, and then place in the fridge to set for at least 1–2 hours.

Turn out if you wish, and decorate with chocolate sauce and a little piped whipped cream.

Chocolate Sauce

*E*specially good with the Irish Mist Mousse opposite, this sauce can be served with many other desserts.

Gently melt together the chocolate, 2 tbsp of the water and the coffee in a small pan. Add the remaining water and the sugar and heat gently, stirring, until dissolved. Simmer uncovered for 10 minutes, then leave to cool.

Serves 4

6 oz (175 g) plain
   chocolate, broken
   into pieces
¼ pint (150 ml) water
1 tsp instant coffee
   powder
4 oz (110 g)
   caster sugar

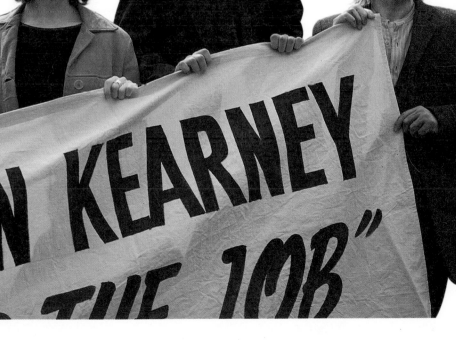

from the
CHURCHES

Religion is an important part of the fabric of rural life in Ireland, and every village has its church. In Avoca, St Mary and St Patrick's – which doubles as St Joseph's in the *Ballykissangel* series – sits above the village, looking down into the river valley below.

Church is a traditional venue on Sundays after a generous Irish breakfast. The primary purpose of going to church is devotion, of course, but, rather like the pub, it's a chance to catch up on the week's news, to review the performance of the local team the day before, and to discuss the all-important weather. It also provides an opportunity to see your neighbours whom you might not have encountered since last Sunday.

All this gossip and rumour-mongering whets the appetite (despite that huge breakfast) for a traditional Sunday lunch, a happy occasion in which the whole family can participate. Often this is a simple roast, with potatoes, vegetables and gravy, followed by an easy pudding. It might, however, be your turn to invite the PP (parish priest) for lunch. If so, it

would have to be a more elaborate affair, as you would not want to be outdone by the preceding Sunday's hosts! *Ballykissangel*'s PP, Father MacAnally, has never shown any enthusiasm for food, although in one episode young Father Peter was treated to a surprise candlelit dinner in his own home. Chances are he would have enjoyed it more if Jenny Clarke, who cooked the meal, hadn't been madly in love with him.

PP Porridge

*O*ur local PP (parish priest) quite often comes over for breakfast. Well, it's not really breakfast, but a large bowl of porridge cooked the way his mother used to make it.

Per person

3 oz (80 g) oatflakes
¼ pint (150 ml) cold
    water
¼ tsp salt
1 tbsp chopped mixed
    nuts
1 tsp honey
1 tsp strawberry jam
1 tbsp light brown
    sugar
pouring cream

In a small pot, mix the oatflakes, water and salt. Leave for a few minutes, then heat slowly until it starts to boil. Simmer for a few minutes. You might need a little more water but our PP likes this consistency.

Remove from the heat and pour into a heatproof bowl. Sprinkle with mixed nuts, and add the honey and jam. Sprinkle with brown sugar and put under a hot grill until the sugar melts and starts to burn. Remove from the grill, pour the cream over, and eat. Best served in the morning.

Sunday Breakfast

Sunday breakfast in Ireland was always a feast. Most households still carry on the tradition, although perhaps not so elaborately as in this recipe.

Serves 4

4 medium tomatoes

4 potato cakes (I lb/ 450 g mashed potatoes, cold or freshly made)

seasoned flour

oil or Irish butter for frying

8 sausages

4 pieces white pudding

4 pieces black pudding

4 breakfast mushrooms

16 button mushrooms

8 back rashers bacon

4 eggs

8 pieces of brown bread for toasting

Preheat the oven to 120°C/250°F/Gas ½. Put 4 plates in to get warm.

Butterfly the 4 tomatoes (cut in half, but not quite through, and open out). Place them on a baking tray and then into the oven.

Make the potato cakes by dividing the mashed potato in four and forming into rounds. Dredge with seasoned flour and fry on both sides until golden brown. Place in the oven.

In a clean pan fry the sausages and puddings until cooked, and place in the oven. Cook the mushrooms in the same way and place in the oven. Clean the pan again and fry the bacon without any fat, then place in the oven.

Fry the eggs. Arrange everything on the plates. Toast the brown bread and stick on the kettle for a cup of tea.

Roast Rib of Beef

Traditionally, Sunday is a family day. Sunday lunch was and still is a celebration, so it was the best meal of the week, often starting with a soup, then a roast, and always a dessert. This was usually prepared by the female members of the family, as the men quite often went from the church to the pub . . .

Cut the meat away from the bone (your butcher will do this for you). Sprinkle with salt and seal the meat in a hot pan in a little oil. Spread mustard all over the meat and place back on the bone in a roasting tray. Place in the preheated oven at 200°C/400°F/Gas 6 for 30 minutes then reduce the heat to 180°C/350°F/Gas 4 and roast for a further hour.

Boil the potatoes in cold salted water for 5 minutes. Drain and place in the oven with the beef for its hour at the lower temperature.

About 15 minutes before the meat has finished cooking, place the whole cauliflower in a pot and boil for 10 minutes. Remove it from the boiling water and drain well. Place on a baking tray, cover with the grated cheese, and put in the oven for 10 minutes until the cheese melts.

Meanwhile, slice the carrots and boil in salted water until tender, a few minutes only. Drain well and keep warm.

Remove the meat and potatoes from the roasting tray when they are ready. Let the meat rest, and keep the potatoes warm. Remove most of the cooking fat from the tray, and add the cornflour and water to the meat juices. Mix with a spatula and bring to the boil. Simmer until slightly thickened. Season with salt and pepper. Pour into a gravy dish and keep hot.

Slice the meat into thick slices and place on serving plates. It should be pink and very tasty. Serve with the roast potatoes, carrots, cauliflower cheese and gravy.

Serves 4

2 beef ribs on the bone
salt and pepper
corn oil
4 tbsp grain mustard
8 potatoes
1 medium cauliflower
1 oz (25 g) Cheddar
   cheese, grated
4 medium carrots

GRAVY
1 tsp cornflour
½ pint (300 ml) water

Curate Casserole

Oddly enough, the curate's housekeeper never works on Sundays, so the parishioners take it upon themselves to feed him in turn. This recipe is one of his favourites.

Serves 4

4 oz (110 g) venison leg
   meat

4 oz (110 g) lean
   stewing beef

1 small hare

2 pigeon breasts

1 oz (25 g) plain flour

2 oz (50 g) Irish butter

1 large onion, peeled

8 medium mushrooms

½ pint (300 ml) beef
   stock

1 pint (600 ml) red
   wine

salt and pepper

a pinch each of dried
   rosemary and thyme

2 garlic cloves, peeled
   and chopped

about 2–4 oz (55–110 g)
   frozen puff pastry,
   depending on the
   size of the dish

1 egg, beaten

Dice the venison and beef, dredge with flour, and brown in some butter in a pan. Remove from the pan and place in a casserole. Remove the meat from the hare, dredge it with flour, brown it in some butter in the pan, and add to the casserole.

Slice the onion and mushrooms and add to the casserole with the stock and wine. Bring to the boil, season with salt, pepper, rosemary and thyme, then reduce the heat and simmer for half an hour. Add the whole pigeon breasts and the chopped garlic. Place the casserole in the preheated oven at 140°C/275°F/Gas 1 for 1½ hours.

Roll out enough pastry to cover the casserole and place on top of the casserole. Brush with egg wash and return to the oven, increased to 200°C/400°F/Gas 6. Bake for 10 minutes until the pastry is golden brown.

Serve with boiled potatoes, carrots and garden peas.

Honey-baked Ham with Brussels Sprouts

*T*his dish is synonymous with Christmas for most Irish people, and it is usually just simply boiled and served with turkey. Cold, it is often one of the meats served at wakes.

Steep the ham in cold water for 3–4 hours or overnight. Rinse the ham and cover with fresh cold water. Bring to the boil and simmer for 2 hours. Remove the ham from the water (which you keep), and place on a baking tray. Remove all the skin and fat. Stud the ham with the cloves and pour the honey and sugar over the top.

Place the ham in the preheated oven at 160°C/325°F/Gas 3 for 45 minutes, spooning the honey mixture over it several times during baking.

Prepare the Brussels sprouts, and place in the ham water. Bring to the boil and hard-boil for 5 minutes. Drain and place in a large pan. Take 2 tbsp of the ham honey mixture and add them to the Brussels sprouts, along with the cream and black pepper. Heat gently and stir until the liquid is absorbed by the Brussels sprouts.

Place the ham in the centre of a large serving plate and surround with the creamy Brussels sprouts. Bring to the table and let your guests feast on the aromas.

Serves 12 very generously (with loads left over)

I whole pale ham (unsmoked gammon) on the bone
30 cloves
8 oz (225 g) honey
4 tbsp dark brown sugar
2¼ lb (1 kg) fresh Brussels sprouts
¼ pint (150 ml) single cream
lots of freshly ground black pepper

Pancakes

Traditionally eaten on Shrove Tuesday, the eve of Lent in the Church calendar. This is a day of feasting before abstaining from something you really like or indulge in (e.g. sweets, chocolate, cigarettes and, of course, the demon drink). The pancakes use up all the butter, sugar, eggs etc. that are left.

The ingredients and consistency of the pancakes varies from house to house, mainly because no one ever knows how many pancakes they have to make. What you have with the pancakes is whatever you fancy – virtually anything!

Serves 4

4 oz (110 g) plain flour
¼ tsp salt
2 eggs, beaten
8 fl oz (250 ml) milk
corn oil

Sieve the flour into a mixing bowl, and make a well in the centre. Add the salt and beaten eggs to the well, then a little milk. Whisk together until thick and creamy, making sure there are no lumps. Add the remaining milk, whisk again, then leave to stand for 30 minutes.

To cook the pancakes, you will need a good heavy-based non-stick pan, a pot of boiling water with a plate on top and a lid, to keep your pancakes hot. Paint a very thin coating of oil on your pan (best done with a basting brush). Pour 3–4 tbsp batter into the centre of the pan. Tilt the pan until it is completely covered. Cook for a minute, or until set, then turn the pancake over (flip if you can), and cook for 30 seconds. Lift out of the pan and place flat on the plate on top of the boiling water, and cover with the lid. Repeat this process until all the batter is gone.

Roll up with lemon juice and a sprinkling of sugar inside, or with ice cream as a dessert, or for tea with butter, jam or honey. You could stuff them with a savoury filling as well.

Brown Bread Ice Cream

This is a good and easy ice cream to make as a pudding after Sunday lunch (and would be good inside a pancake). You can use yesterday's brown bread – if you want to use the Brown Yeast Bread on page 112, toast it first, and then process to crumbs.

Preheat the oven to 180°C/350°F/Gas 4. Spread the crumbs on a baking sheet and bake in the oven until golden brown, about 10 minutes. Shake the tray occasionally. Allow to cool.

Whisk the egg whites until stiff, gradually whisking in the caster sugar. In another bowl whisk the cream to soft peaks. Fold the cool breadcrumbs and whipped cream into the egg whites, adding the vanilla essence. When thoroughly folded, place in a 2 pint (1.2 litre) container, then freeze for 3–4 hours or until firm.

Allow to soften in the fridge for 15 minutes before serving.

Serves 4

4 oz (110 g) brown
   breadcrumbs
4 egg whites
4 oz (110 g) caster
   sugar
1 pint (600 ml) double
   cream
1 tsp vanilla essence

Bailey's Chocolate Mousse Cake

A rich chocolate dessert which would also appeal to the PP or curate after Sunday lunch. It can be made in advance and served straight from the freezer. It is a good way to use up egg yolks if you have made meringues.

Serves 4

8 oz (225 g) plain
  chocolate, or 1 × 6 oz
  (175 g) bar Dairy
  Milk and 2 oz (55 g)
  cooking chocolate,
  broken into pieces

4 oz (110 g) Irish butter

4 oz (110 g) caster
  sugar

4–5 egg yolks,
  depending on size

2 tablespoons Bailey's
  Irish Cream, Irish
  Mist or brandy

¾ pint (450 ml) double
  cream

TO SERVE
cocoa powder
grated chocolate
whipped cream

Using extra butter, grease a piece of parchment paper to fit inside a 9 in (23 cm) springform cake tin.

Melt the chocolate in a bowl over a pan of simmering water. Put the butter, sugar, egg yolks, Bailey's and melted chocolate into a food processor or blender. Mix well for about 3–4 minutes. Whip the cream to soft peaks.

Transfer the chocolate mixture to a large mixing bowl and fold in the whipped cream. Pour the mixture into the prepared cake tin and place in the freezer overnight.

Serve straight from the freezer. Decorate with cocoa powder and some grated chocolate and serve with a little whipped cream and a Hazelnut Biscuit (see page 72), as we did in the photograph on pages 116–17.

Index